EXPERIENCING DIVERSITY

THOUGHT AND PRACTICE
SECOND ANNUAL YEARBOOK
OF THE BANK STREET COLLEGE OF EDUCATION
1994

Editors:
Frank Pignatelli, Susanna W. Pflaum
Board of Advisers:
Nancy Balaban, Harriet Cuffaro, Barbara Dubitsky,
Linda Levine, Maritza McDonald, Susanna W. Pflaum,
Sylvia Ross, Steven Schultz, Edna Shapiro, Bernice Wilson
Readers:
Nancy Balaban, Marvin Cohen, Barbara Dubitsky, Helen Freidus,
Lonnetta Gaines, Lisa Garrison, Lia Gelb, Claudia Grose,
Mary Hilles, Marian Howard, Nina Jaffe, Nina Jensen,
Kenneth Jewell, Fern Khan, Joseph Kleinman, Linda Levine,
Leah Levinger, Claudia Lewis, Nancy Nager, Katherine O'Donnell,
Madeleine Ray, Esther Rosenfeld, Sylvia Ross, Gil Schmerler,
Steven Schultz, Edna Shapiro, Jo Straceski, Susan Sullivan,
Nola Whiteman, Bernice Wilson, Claire Wurtzel

EXPERIENCING DIVERSITY

Toward Educational Equity

Editors:
Frank Pignatelli
Susanna W. Pflaum

CORWIN PRESS, INC.
A Sage Publications Company
Thousand Oaks, California

For information address:

Corwin Press
A Sage Publications Company
2455 Teller Road
Thousand Oaks, California 91320

SAGE Publications Ltd.
6 Bonhill Street
London EC2A 4PU
United Kingdom

SAGE Publications India Pvt. Ltd.
M-32 Market
Greater Kailash I
New Delhi 110 048 India

Printed in the United States of America

Library of Congress Cataloging-in-Publication Data

Main entry under title:

Experiencing diversity: toward educational equity/editors, Frank
Pignatelli, Susanna W. Pflaum.
    p. cm.—(Thought and practice)
  Includes bibliographical references and index.
  ISBN 0-8039-6142-1 (cloth : alk. paper).—ISBN 0-8039-6143-X
(pbk.: alk. paper)
    1. Educational equalization—United States. 2. Minorities—
Education—United States. 3. Multicultural education—United
States. I. Pignatelli, Frank. II. Pflaum, Susanna W.
III. Series: Thought and practice; v.1
LC213.2.E97   1994
370.19'341—dc20   94-7438

94 95 96 97 98   10 9 8 7 6 5 4 3 2

Corwin Press Production Editor: Diane S. Foster

Contents

Preface

FRANK PIGNATELLI

SUSANNA W. PFLAUM

Americans have always relied on the power of schools to address the troubling, long-standing disparities of income and social status that remain deeply entrenched in the society at large, most crucially in the inner cities. "Education," Myrdal observed in 1944, "has always been the great hope for both individual and society. In the American Creed it has been the main ground upon which 'equality of opportunity for the individual' and 'free outlet for ability' could be based" (quoted in Tyack & Hansot, 1982, p. 224). Yet pockets of poverty grow and large metropolitan areas are imperiled. Visions of what might be recede ever faster from the social horizon and memory. Those most in need of realizing lives different from those they now live, those who have no choice but to rely upon the schools to provide alternatives, experience the failure of promises of equal opportunity and diminishing expectations.

Educational reformers often organize their response as a call to provide equal opportunity for all. But although the image of a level playing field may be appealing, a disquieting subtext remains. What about those who fail to rise out of their circumstances once given their opportunity? How far can we stretch

EDITORS' NOTE: We want to thank Mimi Fahnestock and staff of the Bank Street Library for their help in preparing features of this book.

the principle (or is it a useful myth?) of equal opportunity? For example, can democratic habits of equal participation carefully nurtured in some of our better schools extend beyond the relatively safe confines of these schools? Indeed, to fix the eye of reform on "opportunity," using a norm that never has existed for those most in need, risks loosing sight of the actual experiences and the embedded habits, attitudes, and modes of relating that in effect contribute to producing inequality.

Educational reformers must remain attentive to the voice of the child/family/community that is poor, culturally or linguistically different, handicapped; otherwise they will achieve no reform. They must think and *listen* with care. They must attend to opening up spaces where those in less pressing circumstances see the need and develop the skills to dialogue across differences of class, race, and culture, differences that feed harsh relations of power and fix patterns of neglect. They must do this without permanently fixing the label of victim on some and victor on others. The focus on Western history, literature, and the arts disadvantages the children of people from non-Western traditions as it does those from the mainstream. The labeling and placement of students thought to be incapable of learning in "regular" classrooms inhibits their potential not only in academic learning but also in self-knowledge; concomitantly, students in the "regular" classes do not experience the diversity that is really present in the public school systems and learn to equate difference with deficit, missing, at the least, the chance to find common cause with an unexpected friend. Equity is a move to attend to the actual outcomes of schooling and to the real effects of reform on the lives of those in whose interests educators act.

From various vantage points equity issues in education and the conditions out of which they emerge frame the chapters of this second annual Bank Street College of Education Yearbook of Thought and Practice. Several of the authors employ or look toward the narrative form to shape their concerns and press their arguments (Kohl, Wickens with Schultz, Barnes, Goodman, Penberg, Rosenfeld). Kohl, for example, is drawn to both fiction and episodes in his own past as an activist. Barnes, an ethnographer, centers her discussion about equity around a comment by a Latina principal during an evaluation she and other "outsiders" conducted. "Did you notice," the principal says to Barnes offhandedly about members of the evaluation team, "that they didn't eat?" It is the entwining of cultural indifference and power that Barnes wants to draw our attention to; how a dominant culture carries and maintains asymmetrical relations of power. For Goodman the opportunity to address the issue of equity was framed by an investigation by recently graduated high school students of the stark differences in material resources and cultural capital discovered in two public schools within the same school district in New York City. The student documentary provides glaring evidence of systematic disparities, but it is the story of the *making* of the documentary he tells here. As he puts it: "The narrative of the making of this documentary carries within it the story of how, through the conscious act of creation, students make meaning of the world around them, and in turn, reshape themselves and their communities." For Goodman, equity meant posing "the problem of their own educations" to these young people and providing them with support to answer their own questions. Similarly, Wickens with Schultz, teacher educators and advisers, are prodded to examine the issue of equity by a question posed by a student, a first-year teacher who asked, "I will have a child in my class with two moms, two lesbians. What do you know about this?"

In all these cases, equity presents itself, as it were, as a challenge to respond to a felt need; it emerges as a timely answer, a thoughtful caring. Kohl writes, "equity is a matter of values." Equity presumes that moral purpose in addition to intelligent management of resources must guide educational choices. In matters of equity, formulaic responses removed from the exigencies of real life involve complexity, rupture, complication. To respond to the needs of the poor, for example, which Greer states is necessary for real reform, a fairer distribution of resources is needed (with some districts receiving smaller state allocations, a point of serious dispute in some states).

Inequitable conditions betray a lack of regard for the other and often this absence or nonrecognition remains sedimented in the form as well as the content of curriculum. Inclusion, therefore, becomes a strong consideration. Along these lines, Dubitsky with Eilenfeldt, Metnetsky, and Morales discuss work in mathematics leadership for women teachers and efforts to motivate girls to enjoy and actively participate in mathematics; Wickens with Schultz describe how teachers and administrators can respond and have responded to nonmainstream family structures; and Kohl addresses the profound harm done to children and their families by a lack of cultural visibility in the schools they attend. Whatever the arena, it is the combination of our tendency to strongly affirm equality (by which is meant equal opportunity in the job market) and our maintaining structures that simultaneously preserve inequity that makes it difficult to create change. Within this arena of tension lie several dilemmas that are addressed in this book.

One has to do with participation in decisions affecting schools. When decisions about resources, curriculum, assignment of students to classes, and organization are made—as they are— by educators, possibilities are more often than not limited to the manipulation of a closed set of variables that too often exclude consideration of change predicated upon equity. More specifically, as Aronowitz argues, schooling is presently facing a legitimacy crisis for growing numbers of disaffected inner-city youth. Too often embedded in a corporate rhetoric of national competitiveness and economic survival, school reform efforts intended to bridge the widening gap between schooling and future prospects in the workplace risk evading more fundamental and enduring educational issues. These are issues, Aronowitz argues, that educators have vastly more control over than is realized, namely, to engender and support a love of learning for its own sake and as a matter of personal development, to nurture and provide structures and space for the practice of active participation by students in the life of the school they attend and the communities they inhabit. In this same vein, Greer looks critically at the forces behind a system of privatized school choice, a corollary of supply side economic thinking. He argues that we risk the further erosion of our democratic culture if this "privatization paradigm" widens its influence nationally and expands deeper into the inner cities. He, too, has deep reservations about the power of schooling to affect changes in economic opportunities for the poor. Greer does, however, see hopeful signs, if educators take up the challenge to rethink what they mean by, and how they practice, democratic schooling. Both he and Aronowitz are concerned about the necessary but enfeebled links between schooling, self-development, and civic responsibility that exist in schools of, and for, the poor. In Rosenfeld's chapter, we get a close look at how one educator goes about framing these kinds of concerns and building such a school.

This press toward maintenance raises issues around who is involved in making important decisions (Aronowitz) and in evaluation and assessment (Barnes). Without substantial participation by family and community members as well as creative members of the various professional groups involved with schools in decision making, promises of equity will remain empty, unfulfilled. How to organize a broad-based, systemic effort along the lines suggested here and how to sustain the participation of interested constituencies among those who have a stake in the lives and education of children is a dilemma still before us. The possibility of chipping away at the structural and cultural conditions that produce widely varying degrees of opportunity just might be enhanced if the public school can become a locus for the development of a democratic citizenry. Both Greer and Aronowitz point to examples of such undertakings and speculate about how to proceed with such an agenda.

Throughout these chapters one finds questions about whose voices ought to be represented. Indeed, the question of speaking, listening, and audience underlies several of the papers. Kohl relies on story to represent the experience of a community of parents objecting to aspects of their children's school and to present the vision of what can be. Barnes analyzes the issue of spokesperson and audience in terms of school evaluation. Wickens with Schultz use the stories of teachers and parents to draw us into the dilemmas of family structure and school responsiveness. Goodman presents his students' reactions to and learning from their work in the schools while videotaping. Penberg presents the stories of youths engaged in learning outside school. There are other stories; to listen to these stories is to gain appreciation of the complexity of and urgency for reform toward equity.

The role of work for secondary students is explored in two chapters, highlighting a potential dilemma. Both Aronowitz and Greer discuss work in the context of equity. The concept of work while learning is an interesting ground for testing approaches for realizing equity. Greer lauds the potential of internships for providing experience for later work; internships are one of several suggestions of programming possible for youth that build on current status and need. On the other hand, although he agrees that the work options are limited for undereducated students in today's schools, Aronowitz questions whether work activities such as internships ought to be thought of as leading to adult work. Rather, work and activity outside of school lead to extended study and exploration. The experiences Goodman describes his video makers having as they explore resource difference furnish a powerful example. Certainly, service requirements in many elite schools are not meant to lead to careers; rather they are to be an integral part of development toward enlightened citizenship and the experience of participation. Widespread application of the internship model for poor students must not become a further means for separating the experiences of mainstream and nonmainstream students.

Another dilemma has to do with provision of appropriate education for children and youth who do not fit easily into mainstream classrooms and school structures, children with special needs (Wolfe), those for whom English is not the first language (Romero), and the children of gay- and lesbian-headed households (Wickens with Schultz). In each case, tension exists between educational responses to difference and the need to broaden definitions of what students hold in common.

For 77 years the Bank Street College of Education has professed and realized models of progressive education, changing and developing. Since the early 1960s when it was a leader in the development of Head Start, later in Follow Through, and subsequently in many different projects and activities, Bank Street has sought solutions to issues of equity. This volume represents its further commitment to the question.

The chapters in this volume analyze the several arenas in which our society must seek greater equity. They do not offer a blueprint, for indeed, if change requires the participation of teachers, family, and community, there can never be any single answer. They do not even offer a singular theory or body of literature. Rather, and in keeping with the traditions of inquiry and exploration, they offer several paths for thought and action. We hope readers feel they have profited from engaging in these paths.

Reference

Tyack, D., & Hansot, E. (1982). *Managers of virtue: Public school leadership in America, 1820-1980.* New York: Basic Books.

About the Authors

Stanley Aronowitz is Professor of Sociology and Director of the Center for Cultural Studies at the City University of New York Graduate Center. He is the author of 10 books, including *Postmodern Education* and *Education Under Siege*, both coauthored with Henry Giroux. His most recent book is *Roll Over Beethoven: The Return of Cultural Strife* (Wesleyan University Press).

Nancy Barnes teaches cultural anthropology at Lang College, the New School for Social Research. She is currently involved in several collaborative projects with New York City high schools and teaches in the Senior Institute at Central Park East Secondary School.

Barbara Dubitsky directs the Mathematics Leadership Program and chairs the Computers in Education Program at Bank Street College of Education. She has taught mathematics and computer courses at Bank Street College for the past 15 years and designed innovative mathematics curricula, materials, and software for elementary school children and teachers.

Phyllis Eilenfeldt has been a teacher of mathematics for 14 years and is currently teaching in the Young Adult Learning

Academy (YALA). She holds a M.F.A. in sculpture and is a student in the Mathematics Leadership Program.

Steven Goodman studied at the Columbia Graduate School of Journalism and is Founder-Director of the Educational Video Center (EVC), a nonprofit media center for empowering inner-city youth with training and support services in documentary production and media analysis. He produced and directed *Shotgun,* a documentary portrait of a South Bronx youth gang member, and he and his students have worked on many films. Most recently, he was the executive producer for the EVC documentary *Unequal Education: Failing Our Children,* which aired on the Bill Moyers PBS series, "Listening to America." He is a board member of the National Council of Teachers of English Commission on Media, the National Alliance of Media Education, and the Media Alliance.

Colin Greer is President of the New World Foundation. He is the author of *The Great School Legend* and coauthor of *Choosing Equality* and *The Case for Democratic Schooling,* which won the American Library Association's Intellectual Freedom Award in 1988. He was a Professor at City University of New York for 11 years, where he developed new programs for teacher training and for students with learning problems. In the 1970s, he worked on a series of urban school evaluation projects. He is on the editorial boards of *Education and Equity, Tikkun,* and *Social Policy* and serves as a consultant to government, publishing, and television on issues of education and immigration.

Herbert Kohl is a teacher, writer, and education activist. Over the past 30 years he has taught all grades from kindergarten through graduate school. Among his books are *36 Children, Half the House, On Teaching, Growing Minds,* and *From Archetype to Zeitgeist.* His latest book, *I Won't Learn From You and Other Essays,* will be published by the New Press next winter.

Linda Metnetsky teaches "Math for Teachers" at Bank Street College. She also teaches junior high school mathematics at the

Woodward School and consults to public and private schools in the New York metropolitan area.

Michelle Morales has been a kindergarten teacher at P.S. 144 for 4 years. She is a mathematics leader in Bank Street's Mathematics Leadership Collaboration.

David Penberg directed the Liberty Partnership at Bank Street since from 1989 to 1993. He has directed a community center in East Harlem and coordinated a demonstration project on critical thinking and computers at the Door. He is also a cross-cultural educator and has taught in the People's Republic of China and in Bogota, Colombia. He is a doctoral student at the University of British Columbia in Vancouver.

Susanna W. Pflaum is Dean, Graduate School, Bank Street College of Education. Prior positions have included Dean, School of Education, Queens College, CUNY and faculty and administrative positions at the University of Illinois, Chicago. Her publications include books and research papers on reading behaviors of learning disabled children, language development, and teacher education. She is concerned about issues of equity and access in schooling and teacher preparation. With Frank Pignatelli, she coedits the *Thought and Practice* series.

Frank Pignatelli is an Instructor and Advisor on the faculty of Bank Street College Graduate School, Department of Educational Leadership. Prior positions include Adjunct Professor at City College of the City University of New York and various positions in the New York City public school system, including social studies teacher at the junior high school level and administrator on the school, district, and central board levels. He received his B.A. and M.A. from City College and his M.Phil. and Ph.D. in philosophy and education from Teachers College, Columbia University. His research interests and publications include the analysis of progressive pedagogy, teacher/administrator as researcher, the application of postmodernist analysis to issues of schooling, urban school reform, and teacher agency. He is coeditor, with Susanna W. Pflaum, of *Celebrating Diverse Voices: Progressive Education and Equity.*

Olga Romero is Chair of Bilingual Programs at Bank Street College of Education. She received her Ph. D. from the Graduate Center of the City University of New York in Speech and Hearing Sciences. Her dissertation explored areas of bilingual language development. Her interest in bilingualism and language disorders has led to her work as an instructor in the areas of language development and disorders, bilingualism, and learning disabilities. She has written, presented, and consulted on topics ranging from learning disabilities in language-minority college students to the role of language interpreters in the evaluation of students.

Herb Rosenfeld retired from the New York City Public School System after service in the secondary schools as a mathematics teacher, school administrator, curriculum developer, and school planner. He helped plan and develop the Manhattan Center for Science and Mathematics High School, cofounded the Central Park East Secondary School, and most recently started the East Side Community High School. He presently is a consultant to several schools and programs in New York City and elsewhere.

Steven Schultz is on the faculty of Bank Street College. He received his M.Ed. from Wheelock College and Ed.D. from Teachers College, Columbia University. He recently coauthored an article on lesbian and gay parents and the schools and is working on a book about communication problems and routes between lesbian and gay parents and the schools. His research interests include children's conceptions of family; the manifestation of, and precursors to, sexual orientation in young children; and hidden curriculum as interpreted by social reproduction and resistance theories.

Elaine Wickens is on the faculty of Bank Street College of Education. Her book *Anna Day and the O Ring* was be published in 1994 by Alyson Press. It is a photographic story of a family with two mothers, their 4-year-old son, and a family dog, Anna Day.

John Wolfe is on the faculty of the Special Education Department at Bank Street College. He began teaching in New York City public schools in 1967. He has directed a small, independent school, worked in day care, and taught for 11 years at Central Park East II. He is a doctoral student in special education at Teachers College. One of his children, Jesse, has "mild-to-moderate" cerebral palsy.

1. Community Education and Education for Community

COLIN GREER

A lot of attention has been given to public education recently, but it is not likely to go far enough unless we recognize how school reform seems perennially to lurch from one crisis to another. In fact it is reasonable to describe the periodic declaration of crisis as a style of management—one that has historically characterized public schooling. In such a system, successive ebbs and flows in public spending have meant minimal progress on the fundamental issues that periodically rise to crisis scale: equity and social justice.

The major flaws in a management-by-crisis approach are (a) continual direction of funds to the symptoms setting the nomenclature of a particular crisis, often disrupting schools' attempts to maintain a consistent focus on a basic educational philosophy and social agenda; and (b) perpetual presentation of the false impression that the problems faced are recent and new. In fact, more than 50% of public school students have always failed academically by whatever standards used by schools at every time since the middle of the 19th century. The poorest in schools have always sustained the highest rates of dropping out and flunking out, although until recently, work opportunities did not seem to be affected by lack of diplomas.

1

This approach is the backdrop against which many are looking to privatization. The recent waves of appeals for privatization hide under the rubric of "choice," but this is quite different from the idea of public schools of choice appropriately endorsed by many progressive educators. Those who argue that the private sector is the solution misguidedly ignore the reality that goals have changed in 150 years of public school history. Public schools are an evolving institution, changing in relation to our nation's economic needs and cultural values. The public schools were first developed at a time in our history when child labor and slavery were legal. Starting with the 19th-century charity schools, moving through what was known as common schools, public schools have evolved to meet the demands of society. Whereas an elementary school education was at one time deemed sufficient for students to enter the work force, now many jobs require at least some college education. For African Americans, immigrants, and the poor, schools have served as the primary source of integration into mainstream society. As society has changed, so have our public schools, and to think of abandoning them because we're encountering new problems is neither responsible, sensible, nor democratic.

A free public education is something most Americans take for granted. But with all the bad news recently about the "failure" in our public schools, more and more attention has been given to the idea that the private sector can solve problems the public sector cannot cope with. Behind this screen of school reform rhetoric, there is a movement to redefine public schooling: presence of "public" dollars, by this definition, equals public education.

With a new administration in Washington, it would seem at first flush that the privatization imperative in education is a thing of the past. In fact, a campaign to privatize human services (including education) is still a live issue in many states. It remains very important to challenge this onslaught because the capacity to deliver equitable educational services to all children will be destroyed (Bastian, Greer, Fruchter, Haskins, & Gittel, 1988; Bowles & Gintis, 1976; Tyack, 1974).

Privatization calls on for-profit corporations to run our schools. If this sounds like fantasy about corporate America, take a look at Educational Alternatives, Inc., which already has contracts to run public schools in Baltimore. In 1992 a bevy of companies like this made proposals to take over public schools or open supermarket schools, often with research and development costs to be underwritten by public dollars.

When he was Secretary of Education during the Bush administration, Lamar Alexander proposed a redefinition that would include the possibility of public schools run by corporations: "Any school to which a child might go," he said, "supported by public funds, answerable to public authorities and regulation, would be a public school whether it is run by the Smithsonian Institution . . . or IBM." IBM has, in fact, been contemplating the idea of starting schools. So, too, has Apple. Burger King already has opened schools—there are "Burger King Academies" in 14 cities. (This is the Burger King that in 1990 paid unprecedented fines following U.S. Department of Labor charges of widespread child labor law violations.) And of course there is the Edison Project, Chris Whittle's ambitious plan for opening 200 for-profit schools by 1996. Whittle hopes eventually to enroll 2 million students in 1000 schools (Chubb & Moe, 1990; Miner, 1993; Schrag, 1993).

Claims of Privatization Advocates

So what is wrong with a little competition for the public schools, one might ask. Maybe Wall Street can succeed where the public sector has failed.

The first question to be addressed is that of public school "failure." It is crucial we acknowledge that the problems we now see result from unprecedented demands on our education system, not from its failure to cope with a job it handled well in the past. (Ironically, if the schools had worked in the past as so many believe, it would have been as public institutions that they were successful.) School "failure" is generally measured in terms of high dropout rates and poor performance levels on standardized tests. During the "Golden Age" (in the first 50 years of the century before we began regarding academic success as significant) we feel we've lost, dropout levels were just as high and school success was based more on issues of socialization and acculturation for the mainly urban, immigrant population. There were plenty of jobs, although mostly of the low-skill, dead-end variety. Only since the end of World War II has the focus changed to student academic achievement. The major academic problems facing our schools, therefore, are relatively new ones—teaching all children how to think critically, to solve problems, to have the flexibility necessary to cope in our rapidly changing society. As we make the transition to a service economy, the schools are called on to change to meet the needs of the society and to prepare a much higher proportion of its students for jobs that require high degrees of literacy and critical thinking. What we are facing is not a shortage of elite trained professionals, but rather a shortage of workers with a moderate level of technological and scientific skills. To evolve in this way the schools also need to change to meet the needs of the communities they serve by attacking the problems of adult illiteracy and unemployment. Because a key predictor of a child's success in school is the income and education level of his or her parents, the schools need to make an unprecedented effort to make sure that education of parents as well as of children is part of their program (Boyer, 1993; Kozol, 1991; Sarason, 1971).

For-profit private school systems are no better able to deal with this challenge than the current public schools. There is no panacea in the cold pecuniary imperative under cover of "public good" rhetoric on behalf of taxpayer-supported private profit. This unjust redistribution of resources will simply solidify inequity despite empty assurances that this will not be the case. Akin to the savings and loan industry deregulation and subsequent bailout, the new private schools will simply marshal public resources in the interest of profit accumulation and competitive advantage. There is no for-profit plan intended to include large numbers of the current school population. Whittle's

Edison plan, for example, anticipates its schools will have no more than 20% of the student body on scholarship. Where will all the rest go to school?

First, who is everybody else? At this point it is necessary to recall once more that although the private school alternative to public education is new, the "failure" of the majority of school-age children and youth is not. Until the late 1940s and early 1950s with the GI Bill of Rights and the Sputnik explosion in education, school failure rates were high, but not a matter of major concern. How will this continuing pattern of failure fare in the world of educational privateers? Imagine the chains of Wal-Mart, GAP, Chemical Bank outlets; consider their floor space, physical capacity, and periodic store closings. Now imagine a school system run along similar lines. Not accounting for closings and with only 20% of the new private school population on scholarship to supplement modest state vouchers, more than 70% of the current public school population would still be in public school or not-for-profit private and parochial schools. Now integrate this in the equation: Parochial schools (currently with by far the majority of students in private schools) are in a period of extensive retrenchment, closing schools and transferring the most difficult students to public schools. Despite all existing and new for-profit school options, the vast majority of all elementary and secondary school children will be in public schools. That's where the rest will go to school; that is where the challenge to educational effectiveness exists; and that's why equity is coterminous with any serious vision of school reform.

Nevertheless, privatization has been framed almost as if choice were exclusively a private sector asset. Framed as if it were an exclusive and fundamental market verity—which it is not—choice supersedes other democratic values (e.g., diversity and inclusiveness) and obfuscates successful public school efforts to meld choice, diversity, and inclusiveness in school offerings; to wit: magnets, satellites, alternatives, and so forth. Choice in public schools can be a useful way to think about these kinds of options and others. But care needs to be taken that the presumptions in the popular use of the word "choice" do not bring with them marketplace conventions and the subliminal confirmation of the argument for profit-making schools. Further, the application of public dollars to private schools (including not-for-profit privates) has had limited experimentation, as in the case of Milwaukee. But little gain can be shown for low-income people at large because the voucher value awarded does not often approach the rapidly rising private school tuition. In fact, by any serious criterion of diversity and citizen participation, the private sector is severely limited—unless of course one considers child labor, for example, and the free choice of parents and children to elect menial labor over education (Coleman, 1981; Hacker, 1984; National Association of Independent Schools [NAIS], 1992).

But if corporate schools take the cream of the most desirable students, public schools will be left with fewer resources to teach the neediest population—the very population that has the highest dropout rate and the lowest test scores. Teachers will be wooed away by enticements like smaller class size, more resources, and better physical plants, things desperately needed in the public schools. Money will have to be spent on advertising the top-notch public school "magnet" programs, which already attract affluent and savvy parents and which often have admission criteria. Schools in poor districts will be left to fend for themselves, having neither the resources nor the appeal to attract new students or enough teachers, and will eventually become little more than prisons for the poor, warehouses of "failure" hidden out of sight, and sadly, out of mind.

The arguments made by the privateers run in two directions. First, the enthusiasts of specific business school models are practical people who believe that for-profit operations can more effectively use the same dollars now spent. Free of regulation and unions, they look to the production of profits and effective schools. Both vouchers and contracting out are examples of this thrust. The argument is as naive as it is self-interested. We need only to look at the for-profit model in nursing homes, national defense, and prisons to know: (a) the bottom line is secured only by reductions in quality, (b) the private-public scale of corruption is more than the sum of corruption in either sector, and (c) the market runs along elitist gradations of quality. Second, privateers argue theoretically rather than practically that some good schools will lead to a general improvement in schooling—a version of a rising dictum that makes little sense if you bother to notice that the majority of schoolchildren are in schools deeply sunk in mud. This theoretical argument posits a very significant transfer of resources from public to for-profit schools, on the grounds that the market must dominate if the stimulus of market choices is to work its magic. This Friedmanesque perspective requires a thoroughgoing transfer of resources that the practical business people in the first argument do not necessarily embrace.

Against such a backdrop, the public school will cease to play a role in community and political life. There will be little incentive to run for school boards and to participate as citizen parents— roles at the heart of our participatory democracy. Advocates of private "choice" often overlook this important function the public school serves. All over the country, schools provide the basis from which communities connect with and participate in the nation's political process. Local school boards are the entry into politics for ordinary citizens who move from PTA to school board office, and quite often, to higher political office. School board elections are also a vehicle of local political participation; in debates over property taxes, school bonds, curricular concerns, and academic standards, citizens learn to express themselves politically. In a very real fashion, school politics are a barometer of the vitality of the nation's electoral democracy.

The privatization paradigm has won a major ideological victory in the last dozen years, and its adherents aim to eliminate federal and state domestic programs except in so far as they are contracted out to or invested in business enterprises. The language of markets, decentralization, choice, and empowerment, as Max Sawicky points out, is not dedicated to "how to devise a better way to deliver services, but how to overcome the political obstacles to cutting public spending 'directly in the public interest'" (1992). The privatization paradigm preaches the indirect benefit to society of the direct support and financing of private initiatives ("private" standing for corporate in this context is a thorny and rhetorical term).

Limits of the Past

To fully understand the problems facing our public schools, one must look at more than declining test scores and dropout rates. One must first let go of the myth of a Golden Age in public schooling. The fact is, in the time posited as that mythical Golden Age, academic success was just one of many variables under consideration; much more critical were the tasks of getting immigrant children off the streets and into the classroom, particularly with the phasing out of child labor. As the school replaced the work site as prime socializer of working-class children, it explicitly took on the characteristics of the workplace. School time was organized with little regard to children's needs or interests. Training for reliable attendance and obedience was far more important. The goals we currently want our schools to address—critical thinking, problem solving, and flexibility of intelligence—were not even introduced into schools until the reforms of the last 20 years. Unfortunately, most of these reforms have been based on the assumption that the system is fundamentally sound and needs only to recapture past achievement.

What we think of as public education's historic achievement in fact applied only to a small proportion of its population; for the rest, the industrial economy was glad to receive graduates who had learned some basic punctuality, language, and repetitive-motion skills. At no time, including the present, have we experienced school breakdown in the preparation of highly trained managers and skilled professionals. Where schools historically succeeded academically, they continue to do so. By World War II demands for a more educated workforce grew apace. By the Sputnik period education had taken on new significance. At the same time, those who previously left school early and new immigrants in the low-paid workforce continued as a class to leave school early—concentrating in cities until the urban poor recently began migrating to suburbs. Today we face high levels of urban and suburban school failure; not new failure but newly extra-urban and newly dysfunctional to the political economy (Sawicky, 1992).

School dysfunctionality is not an isolated phenomenon, but part of a general interregnum in social authority. The school is a battleground for social values, as its perceived breakdown coincides and corresponds with perceptible breakdown in the authority structures of society at large. Value questions that once seemed resolved, such as church versus state, public versus private, community versus individual, are newly reopened, and the uncertainty with which we as a society explore these tensions is loudly expressed in the context of public education, where we have long sought to resolve value conflicts and transmit shared values across generations. When immigrants came to American cities and looked for a variety of paths to economic mobility and security, the schools were positioned to take credit for any success that was achieved while concentrating on their assimilation functions. The school symbolized advance over manual labor, and staying in school was, so the belief went, preparation for promised white-collar security. It was in this context that the school became synonymous with social progress as well as individual advancement.

In the 1950s and 1960s, education issues, primarily desegregation and decentralization, were shorthand for wider social and political concerns. Both desegregation and decentralization underscored the national recourse to public education for dealing with massive labor problems. Those who were still marginal in American life—African Americans, Latinos, immigrants, the unemployed, returning GIs—were to find economic integration into the mainstream by access to public education. Education, it was believed, would prepare people for opportunities. Rarely was it observed that perhaps a picture of an always bountiful America was questionable, or that the central role of academic success represented a significant revision of some previous expectations for public education.

So, public opinion—as well as educators themselves—stressed the past success of schools as the model to be emulated, thereby passing blame for the schools' failure onto the students, their teachers, and their families. The new concern for academic performance—for all, including the children of the poor—seemed to reveal a new failure of schools to work successfully, but in fact they had never been expected to work that way.

The much-romanticized notion that education has made it possible for rich and poor alike to learn all that is necessary to enter the mainstream of American society simply is not true. The popularity of privatized solutions, then, stems from the conviction both that we confront problems of unprecedented scale and that public sector solutions have not been of a scale equal to the perception of the problem. Some further pruning is in order on this point, clearing away the underbrush of this argument so as to expose the woods more clearly. If the argument that schools are really failing is not accurate; if the idea that choice is a private preserve is false; if public choices are increasingly plentiful but not panaceas; if the private sector dangerously conflates the distinction between social goods and consumer goods, between public interest and private profit—how will we grow us an effective public education for the preparation of informed citizens and educated workers?

The growth we need to nurture will be predicated on recognizing that just as the failure rates are long standing, so the imperative to reverse them is relatively recent—beginning in the 1950s and gathering force in the 1970s. This recognition will curtail both simply looking backward for answers and condemning current school personnel as the first to fail. Indeed, instead of being the first to place blame, the people who now teach in our schools are the first for whom professional effectiveness is defined by response to this challenge; they are the first to take it on. School communities—staff and parents—released from the depressed morale that follows from the sense of unprecedented failure can then direct their energies against the powerful negative equation that dominates public schools: that the income and education level of parents predicts academic achievement (the poorer and less educated the family, the less can be expected from their children as students in school).

The logic of this equation runs deep. The educational effects of concentrations of poor people—primarily in central cities and their suburbs, but also in some rural areas—are among the most serious problems facing the American educational system. Research has indicated that in schools serving areas with high poverty rates, the achievement of *all* pupils, not just that of the individuals from poor families, is negatively affected. For example, the average achievement levels of nonpoor children in high-poverty schools has been found to be lower than those of poor children in schools with very low poverty rates. Further, for all children, the educational effects of poverty are much more severe, the greater the concentration and duration of poverty. There will be no improved school system without addressing the needs of the poor (Irwin, 1992; Rotberg, 1993).

Finally, it is important to recognize that schools, public and private (of any kind), do not constitute an autonomous sphere and thus do not exclusively determine the good or bad results we refer to as educational outcomes, which are in large part a measure of social condition. The fact is we will need to create, with the aid of schools, a society ready for equitable, effective, even excellent schools.

Community and Family Cohesion

All the rhetoric of individualism in this country notwithstanding, successful students are the products of intimate interaction and identification with a culturally valued lifestyle. The strengths of working-class and poor Americans are not highly regarded and are not widely noticed. In establishing a learning readiness awareness for school practice it is absolutely crucial that readiness attributes be derived from "local knowledge." Community and family are the contexts in which schools operate—and for middle-class (aspiring) parents these institutions are usually complementary to school life. Indeed, schools work most successfully when this synergy occurs.

The task here is not to advance to a kind of middle-class conformity in which a learning readiness overlay is designed to erase the ethnic and class characteristics of schoolchildren—a latter-day Americanization program like the one that at the turn of the century explicitly sought to win children from their ethnic backgrounds. Instead, a more comprehensive learning readiness goal must be directed to subsuming each community's unique version of the family cohesion model that middle-class America so ardently supports, and thereby to encourage commonality and acceptance, rather than exclusivity and rejection, for "difference."

I do not mean to introduce monolithic social axioms in this discussion. To be sure, neither middle-class nor poor and working-class lifestyles match school expectations and style in any simple manner. Nor indeed is the school necessarily to be regarded as a set of reasonable resources and pressures for learning, even though these connections are so well established that they can be presented almost as if by natural law. But what is true is that school achievement is approached and codified by schools in a set that unifies the reward structure of public education with the reward expectations of the aspiring or successful middle-class parent community. And it is equally true that other kinds of community and family goals can and should develop productive relations with their public schools. The connection between public schools and the educational potential of the communities they serve is not at all a typical phenomenon; indeed its absence is a major factor in the perpetual reproduction of the link between economic insecurity and poverty and school failure. Recognizing the open and dynamic potential for that connection in diverse communities is basic to school reform and the transformation that supports a public education system characterized by widespread achievement.

Public schools are an aspect of life in all communities, but in many they are foreign outposts. Decolonizing the outposts is a necessary prerequisite for reversing the negative relation between social status and school achievement. How to knit the threads of a positive relationship between schools and poor children is the imperative to rethinking and reinventing our public schools. But the task of reinvention, or to use Lawrence Cremin's (1984) term, "transformation," is in fact about all schools and all students. After all, the necessary focus of resources on children and communities in greatest need will depend finally on the determination of more privileged citizens to support it. The competitive edge of achievement in school and in society seems mostly to respond to the claims of national economic necessity. We are used to the argument that we are under-prepared for the modern global economy and therefore need to support an education reform agenda that promises us a competitive workforce to replace old-style industrial labor. Sometimes that argument succeeds in winning new resources. It never succeeds in restructuring the uneven development that characterizes the public education landscape (Cremin, 1984; deLone, 1979; Hacker, 1984; National Board of Inquiry of the National Coalition of Advocates for Students [NBI], 1985).

To achieve universal effective education, we need to evolve the public schools we believe we once had, schools that effectively encourage students to achieve academically regardless of their social condition. But if public schools are to equip students of all origins and backgrounds to function as productively employed citizens who participate fully in our political and economic life, teaching poor students how to take tests is not the answer. Public education must become more responsive to the socioeconomic realities of those it serves. Schools must serve to reverse the tie between low income and poor performance. We have learned from Head Start and I Have a Dream programs that given adequate resources, school success is possible for the least likely pupils.

The schools, both public and private, as they are now structured, operate on a scarcity model based on the principles of competition, individualism, and exclusion. It is as if there were only so much "good education" to go around and therefore the children must compete with each other to get it. Needless to say, children who attend well-equipped schools staffed by an adequate number of good teachers and who have educated parents and siblings to help them outside of school are going to have a tremendous advantage over children who attend over-crowded, understaffed, underequipped schools and whose parents and siblings are poor and illiterate.

The challenge facing public schools today is to conceive of a system based on the concept of educational plenty as opposed to scarcity. The principles of competition, individualism, and exclusion need to be replaced with those of participation, recognition, and inclusion. Every public school must be a school worth "choosing." We know what works in promoting children's learning: small classes, well-trained (and well-paid) teachers, community service, peer teaching, parental support, a clean and safe environment. The choice we are really making, as a nation, is whether or not to embrace or abandon our commitment to education for all. Public schools will continue to exist; will they be havens for learning for all citizens or bleak, prisonlike warehouses for the poor?

Schools for the Poor

Progress in this restructuring requires two strategic foci: one on schools for the poor; the other on all public schools. The first strategy will have elements integral to achieving its particular objective through a strong emphasis on community education; the second involves an approach to schooling for all students based on the challenge of achieving a sense of national community. The goal here is not two separate (more equal) school systems, but a distinction in focus and resource allocation made necessary by the historic concentration of failure among schools in poor communities.

To be sure, some schools in poor neighborhoods "work." The media have focused considerable attention on these schools. And indeed public schooling can be surprisingly successful, playing an essential role in our society as the repository of hope for both parents and students (to a far greater extent than we notice) and the agent for transmission of authority. It is only by finding hope and meaningful authority in their schools that students can avoid the embitterment that so frequently leads them to explode with the anger so many must feel given the dismal opportunities they face. Indeed, civic culture is strained in America, but a quick glance abroad shows it is by no means bankrupt. Public schools are one of the ingredients in the common customs and shared civic awareness that keep our social fabric fairly well knit (Comer, 1980; Edmunds, 1979; Ford Foundation, 1984).

But if schools for poor children are to succeed, then all poor children must have a real chance of upsetting the social and economic legacy they inherit. To do this, the schools must begin to serve the needs of all the members of the community, not just the children. This is not the case when schools operate as if the local world outside the school does not exist or is to be unilaterally defeated and eliminated. The foundation or principle of this approach is community education. The educational role of the school should include the education of its students and the education of the larger community it serves. Community education means multiage and intergenerational education: peer teaching, community service by school students, community service by community residents as educators, and education of adult community residents.

The goal is the achievement of an intense educational relationship between family, community, and school. Participating schools could be required to provide certain services, such as extended day care and mental health services, unless it can be demonstrated that these services are being adequately and conveniently provided to students and their families by other local institutions or agencies. In extending services to adults as well as youngsters, youth and community tutoring programs would be developed in which seniors and teenagers are employed as educational assistants in the education of the very young and of adult members of the community. The helper-therapy principle—through which the tutor gains at least as much as the tutee—will benefit the learning of all. And the producer value of community self-help—through which resources are extended in reach through local decision making and knowledgeable application—will maximize the value of resources. In this framework, bilingual education, school-to-work education, and parenting skills instruction would be provided to adults of all ages, including high school dropouts and unemployed adults. This can take place through a community education approach that provides youth and adult paraprofessional training as well as peer tutoring and community service as preparation of future teachers. In this way, the chance that all students will have schools and teachers evidencing concern about their individual progress and their community's vitality will be greatly enhanced.

My point here is not to present a program, but to offer reminders and illustrations of how community education can be advanced. Several steps from various sources seem worth considering (Boyte, 1988; Carnegie Council on Policy Studies in Higher Education, 1979; Darling-Hammond, 1984; Gerald, 1992; Picket, 1984; Roosevelt Centennial Youth Project, 1984; Zarrow, 1993).

- Secondary schools should focus on improving the transition from school to work. A nationwide high school corps (perhaps in connection with national service plans) should be created. Schooling and work experience need to be complementary and integrated. Training by itself can lead to frustration and cynicism about work because of mismatches between students' acquired skills and low skill demands of most jobs available to young workers. On the other hand, work experience programs without training often prove ineffective, especially for low-income people of color. In addition to linking school and work, the quality of high school students' jobs seems to influence later labor market success substantially. Students with high schools jobs that among other things provide opportunities to work with adults and to develop and use skills in the workplace often experience greater success in the labor market after high school.

- A key problem with most current elementary and secondary schools is that they fail to prepare disadvantaged students adequately—especially those who do not intend to enter a traditional, 4-year college program—for the transition from school to work. High school partnerships with community organizations can be the basis of apprenticeships or other training programs that develop specific job skills as well as broader, positive work habits and attitudes. All this can be harnessed for academic credit to be applied in the last 2 years of high school or for advanced placement for college once a certification process has been established and a sufficient standard is met (with great benefit in the reduction of college tuition).

- The school-based management approach can maximize the ability of school staff to respond creatively and effectively to pupil and community needs. In addition, a portion of the school's capital budget could be set aside to hire people from the local neighborhood to fill school jobs. A service line could be established by schools, as some teacher unions now do, for parents to call for aid as they themselves try to help their children with homework. The school should be open more hours and through the summer to meet the needs of parents and older siblings who have dropped out of school. It is especially important to develop programs for older children, who will soon be parents themselves. Again it is illusory to think only about working with younger children; putting a child into an early childhood program won't do much good if his or her parents and siblings are poor and illiterate. The power of that local knowledge will be far greater than the impact schools alone can achieve.

- We need to think creatively about our schools to turn problems into solutions. Rather than lamenting teenage pregnancy and adopting a moral stance opposing it, why not extend the programs built around parenting skills? These students could be part of the teacher corps. Involved in infant and early childhood care in this way, the young parents and parents-to-be would learn how to give their children the preschool learning support taken for granted in middle-class homes; two generations could be helped simultaneously. And by taking advantage of the conscientiousness that often accompanies the onset of parenthood a new source of teacher recruitment (especially in communities of color where teacher numbers are diminishing) will have been identified.

- A great deal of international research on immigrants has focused recently on how beneficial to a just society it is to recognize the strengths immigrants bring and the importance of matching these strengths in sectors of need through education and placement programs. Our schoolchildren and their parents (so often recent graduates or dropouts of those same schools) can be recognized as such a resource too. In this way, the anonymity that often characterizes student life can be reversed, a solid self-esteem established, and the pressing problem of teacher recruitment (most serious in and from poor communities and those of color in particular) can be addressed early.

- There is already growing and promising experience involving community-based organization (CBO) partnerships with public schools—through which community organizations invent schools that build community need and resources into the schools' vision, governance, and curriculum. Partnerships with CBOs like American Committee for Reform Now (ACORN), Brooklyn chapter, in New York City and Industrial Areas Foundation (IAF) in Baltimore have begun relationships of this kind. Through these partnerships it might also be possible to stimulate microenterprise development aimed at physically rebuilding badly deteriorated schools or building new schools to reduce scale and class size. This could happen through government grants and partnerships with local banks wishing to improve their performance under the Community Reinvestment Act (which requires loans to poor communities) by matching federal loans.

- Community service programs, increasingly popular throughout the country, can link students with adults and their communities to provide services from which they can learn both academic and job-related skills. In addition, volunteer-initiated service programs at the neighborhood level can be encouraged through partnerships with national and local nonprofits. In this way, a local nonprofit can serve both as administrative agent and mentor to young people pursuing service problem solving as part of their own education. A number of examples already exist. The Federation for Southern Cooperatives (Georgia) and Children of War (Los Angeles) are two promising cases in point. But increased public funds in support of these kinds of programs are needed.

- Better schools—schools that take on the challenge of historic failure—will require public investment, more money. It is essential that schools be equitably funded, which means that although control of the school should be decentralized, responsibility for school budgets should not be. Despite all the rhetoric to the contrary, we continue to spend too little on public schools; in fact, little new money has been invested in general public education improvements since the middle 1960s. All schools need to have adequate funds to hire teachers, to create programs suited to their students, to hire local community members for nonteaching jobs, to supply students, and to maintain a decent physical environment.

Schools for All

Most schools in the United States fail to provide adequate education for their students. My definition of "adequate" rests on the proposition that our schools currently reward achievement in direct relation to failure rather than success. The resulting yardstick, both within individual schools and across schools, reverberates throughout the system as a tacit social requirement for educational disadvantage. And this tradition is routinely and intergenerationally reproduced to make our general schooling socially inadequate.

Our national community is in great distress, too—and all our schools suffer from and reflect it. Equity must be a goal of the nation-as-community and we must educate our children accordingly. That means attention to education in democratic values and equal attention to reducing and removing the education for fear (of failure and subsequent joblessness on graduation), frustration (because curricula seldom dovetail with any desired or available social role), and competition (because success for some is predicated on the failure of others in school and beyond) that pervade our best schools and those that aspire to that status.

The nation-as-community must be at the heart of the education we provide for our children, including those in our successful schools where the sense of community is withered by our reliance on monolithic expectation of proficiency and by the disquieting reality that divergent learning patterns defy the acquisition of school skills. As Richard Westheimer puts it, "to sell short any one child or group of children by expecting too little or demanding unreasoned conformity inhibits and weakens our entire system of education" (1993).

I would like to see a Community Service Learning Act such as has been proposed by several educators (most recently, Kyle Haver of New York City's District 4) that provides for the flexible integration of all other funds and programs in the service of school revitalization and of movement toward a sense of national community—the necessary condition for the democratic awakening struggling to spring forth in local communities, where diversity is not always associated with tolerance and justice.

Vocational education, instead of being a separate "track," should be included in all children's education until at least 10th grade, so that those who choose to pursue the track are prepared to do so and those who take another track at least have an understanding of and respect for the skills involved. The vocational work could be done in the community, with students serving in both blue- and white-collar jobs, learning the skills that it takes to make a community work.

We must claim citizenship as a key school goal and a central component of the curriculum. We live in an increasingly complicated world, and the issues voters have to consider are much more complex than in the past. Schools must consciously serve future voters, teaching how to participate in democracy; and they must—perhaps through their students—reach community members and parents to educate them into the political process by becoming involved in parent associations or running for school boards.

We must embrace the multiculturalism of our nation. That means developing a curriculum that recognizes the diversity of our society and the worth of human beings from all cultures without placing value judgments on any. To do this we must bring students and parents into meaningful contact with those they must now regard as "other."

Finally, testing needs to be developed that is performance based and rooted in democratic values and community needs as well as personal goals. The emphasis on test results is counterproductive unless clearly tied to diagnostic applications. In some schools, much of the school year is spent drilling students on answering test questions. This reinforces competitiveness and undermines understanding; shorn of meaning, schooling becomes little more than an endurance trial in which students and schools grimly and dutifully strain to outlast each other. The current administration's strong emphasis on national academic standards and curricular goals comes perilously close to crisis management. Demanding higher standards means crisis management unless closely tied to a teacher recruitment and training program built to represent a multicultural nation and to serve a wide diversity of learning needs. Without the "access to performance" implicit in these concerns, higher standards will too often mean teaching to tests rather than producing better schooling. Sound academic standards are a crucial element in school accountability, one that those we think of as "better schools" easily meet. But in truth, tests are not the full measure of academic achievement, and what they do measure (to the extent we accept that as a benchmark) will not be advanced on a massive scale unless the school-community setting becomes the paramount context for long-term and deep-rooted change.

In privileged as well as impoverished school-community settings, community-based partnerships are quite complex. The dangers of self-interest, parochialism, and bigotry are great. Witness any school tax battle or the recent resistance in New York City, for example, to a multicultural "rainbow" curriculum. Local partnerships, implicit and successful in some school-community settings, explicit and promising in others, must be subject to more than academic standards. The regulation of public education has to be better thought through and more visionary than that. What we value and need as a society is not limited to how well our kids read and compute. Just as academic adequacy without decent jobs is a dead end, so education defined narrowly as job preparation and economic opportunity with little regard to tolerance, cooperation, and democratic values will further tear at our social fabric. We cannot and should not legislate morality; we should—as with the school desegregation that is still to be achieved—commit our schools to high standards of civility, participation, and industry.

Conclusion

Education is not a zero-sum game. *All* our citizens need to learn not only to read and write, but to think critically in order to participate responsibly in a democratic society, to have the flexibility necessary to meet the demands of a rapidly changing job market, and to live comfortably in a multicultural society. Our public schools struggle with these demands. Further, it is crucial to remember that public schools successfully produce the scientists, engineers, and other professionals we need and many of the skills the current workplace requires; they do not, however, provide those opportunities widely enough or on an equitable basis. Crisis management will not meet these challenges. But if we proceed on the same old reform basis, the education privateers will be waiting in the wings to use the inevitably disappointing results to escalate their demands for for-profit education available only to those with the cash to buy it.

References

Bastian, A., Greer, C., Fruchter, N., Haskins, K., & Gittel, M. (1988). *Choosing equality: The case for democratic schooling.* Philadelphia: Temple University Press.

Bowles, S., & Gintis, H. (1976). *Schooling in capitalist America.* New York: Basic Books.

Boyer, E. (1993). *Ready to learn: A mandate for the nation.* Princeton, NJ: Carnegie Foundation for the Advancement of Teaching.

Boyte, H. (1988). *Community is possible.* New York: Harper & Row.

Carnegie Council on Policy Studies in Higher Education. (1979). *Giving youth a better chance: Options for youth, work and service.* San Francisco: Author.

Chubb, J., & Moe, T. (1990). *Politics, markets, and America's schools.* Washington, DC: Brookings Institution.

Coleman, J. S. (1981). *Coleman report on public and private schools: The draft summary and eight critiques.* Arlington, VA: Education Research Service.

Comer, J. (1980). *School power: Implication of an invention project.* New York: Free Press.

Cremin, L. (1984). *The transformation of the school.* New York: Vintage.

Darling-Hammond, L. (1984, April). *Beyond the commission reports: The coming crisis in teaching* (Report to the Rand Corporation).

deLone, R. H. (1979). *Small futures: Children, inequity, and the limits of liberal reform.* New York: Harcourt Brace Jovanovich.

Edmunds, R. (1979, October). Effective schools for the urban poor. *Educational Leadership, 37*(1), 15-18, 20-24.

Ford Foundation. (1984). *City high schools: A recognition of progress.* New York: Author.

Gerald, D. E. (1992). *Projections of education statistics to 2003* (National Center for Educational Statistics, NCES 92-218). Washington, DC: U.S. Department of Education.

Hacker, A. (1984). The schools flunk out. *New York Times Book Review.*

Irwin, P. M. (1992). *Federal education funding trends: A perspective.* Washington, DC: Congressional Research Service, Library of Congress.

Kozol, J. (1991). *Savage inequalities: Children in America's schools.* New York: Crown.

Miner, B. (1993). Education for sale. *Rethinking Schools, 7*(4), 1, 14-17.

National Association of Independent Schools. (1992). *NAIS statistics.* Boston: Author.

National Board of Inquiry of the National Coalition of Advocates for Students. (1985). *Barriers to excellence: Our children at risk.* Boston: Author.

Picket, A. L. (1984). The paraprofessional movement: An update. *Social Policy, 13*(3), 40-43.

Roosevelt Centennial Youth Project. (1984). *A policy blueprint for community service and youth employment.* Washington, DC: Author.

Rotberg, I. C. (1993). *Federal policy options for improving the education of low-income students.* Rand Institute on Education and Training.

Sarason, S. (1971). *The culture of the school and the problem of change.* Boston: Allyn & Bacon.

Sawicky, M. (1992). What is NEWP? A guiding theory of the right wing. *Social Policy, 22*, 7-19.

Schrag, P. (1993). The great school sell-off. *American Prospect, 12*, 34-43.

Tyack, D. B. (1974). *The one best system.* Cambridge, MA: Harvard University Press.

Westheimer. R. (1993). (Support material for school support report for Senator Wellstone.)

Zarrow, J. (1993, May). *School equity and legislative options: A report for Senator Paul Wellstone.*

2. A Different Perspective on Educational Inequality

STANLEY ARONOWITZ

In the United States, we seem to be permanently wedded to the idea that the credentialing system of public and private education is the primary vehicle through which any student, regardless of race, class, gender, or even physical handicap, may succeed in achieving professional or technical status. If not the great leveler, as Lawrence Cremin (1969) claims, schools perhaps more than other institutions embody for most Americans the fulfillment of the doctrine of equality of opportunity. The key institutional variables, according to this common sense, are the extent of public funding for schools, the rigor and the relevance of the curriculum, and the pertinence and expertise of pedagogy. The underlying assumption of this scenario is that jobs are plentiful for the professionally or technically trained, credentialed worker.

Until the 1980s most educational debates turned on which of these factors was the most important for fulfilling the promise of equal opportunity for working-class and poor kids. "Modern" liberals insisted that student performance—the key variable in occupational mobility—was crucially and causally linked to the limited access of urban schools to both institutional and financial resources in comparison to private and suburban schools. These privileged schools were often rewarded for their affluence by state laws allocating funds by enrollment and attendance. In any case, even suburban public schools are able to draw funds and services from their middle-class and upper-class parent organizations. In contrast to most urban schools, in which the voluntaristic tradition is typically weak, private and suburban schools can, even with the expansion of women in the paid labor force, count on parents for math and reading tutoring, assisting with trips, raising funds, and performing a myriad of other unpaid tasks. Needless to say, the resource imbalance was exacerbated by the fiscal crisis of the states that began to cut deeply into school funds in the 1970s.

"You can't solve school problems by throwing money at education," argued conservative educators who rode the tide of the Reagan revolution. This truism conveniently jibed with the traditional conservative antipathy to social spending, and particularly federal support for education. The superiority of private schools was considered a force of nature, not only on account of the profit motive for their proprietors but also for their reliance on voluntarism. But even with a new Democratic national administration, the doctrine of privatization shows few signs of abating. Meanwhile, in the 1980s, the educational debate nearly abandoned funding considerations as the very concept of a federal education policy came under attack, including federal aid for public schools.

Under prodding from the Heritage Foundation, right-wing intellectuals, such as Chester Finn,[1] and neoliberals, curriculum issues partially displaced other considerations. The educational right demanded a new focus on the three Rs, reinvigorated the almost discredited phonics technology for teaching reading, and mounted what by the mid-1980s seemed an inexorable campaign to reintroduce "values" into the elementary and secondary curricula, not the least of which were those of work, family, and patriotism. They argued that the tonic for the failed urban public schools was to tie education more closely to the labor market than ever before. Education for the vast majority should be transformed into training in marketable skills. Corporations should be recruited to sponsor schools, and in the bargain, advise them as to just what marketable skills are needed for a 21st-century economy. For the elite, the conservatives insisted on the revitalization of the liberal arts on the premise that the antitraditionalism of the 1960s had brought havoc to the curriculum and resulted in an undereducated middle class.

On the cultural front—which spilled over into education—High Culture made a roaring comeback. The NEA and NEH were captured by the ideological right during the Bush administration, and with the Mapplethorpe affair, made it clear that crucial innovations of the artistic avant-garde no longer had a place in the pantheon of federal support for the arts, which in any case came under sharp attack from critics such as Senator Jesse Helms.[2]

But the curriculum struggle took an unexpected turn. After being largely defeated on the fiscal battleground, the educational left (as distinct from the ideological left) counterattacked in two directions: It introduced the "multicultural curriculum," an attempt to broaden the canon to include women's, African American, and Latino cultures. What may be described as "excluded" literature, history, and popular forms were to be integrated into the canon, or according to some, replace it. This effort raised the traditional question of high versus low culture, and especially the relative virtues of teaching "universal" Western values and culture associated with the work of "dead, white males" and what became known as the educational expression of identity politics. Latinos and African Americans posed a new concept—cultural citizenship—against the nationalism of the prevailing political climate and were able to win significant victories if not complete hegemony even as the conservative attack against "political correctness" reached a point of near frenzy at the end of the Bush administration.[3] The success of multiculturalism, cultural studies, and other movements of the new pluralism may be measured by Irving Kristol's rueful admission that the alliance of conservatives and liberals that had been forged to bring the academy in line with the collapse of communism had, at least at the cultural level, lost (Kristol,

1989). Needless to say, his white flag notwithstanding, the battle goes on: The former Reagan speechwriter Pat Buchanan has formed a new group to wage the holy war against the cultural radicals and there is a new mood of retrenchment within universities, expressed sometimes as fiscal restraint and other times in more directly repressive terms, as in the attempt by the administration of the University of Minnesota to dissolve its Humanities department and in the new assault on the liberal arts that pervades many state colleges and universities, including the California State University system and New York's City University.

Take the following information as a basis for discussion. Only 50% of students entering high school graduate. In some New York, Chicago, and Los Angeles high schools, only about 20% graduate; in the middle-class suburbs the number is closer to 75% or 80%. What accounts for the discrepancy (New York City Board of Education, 1992)?

Many contend that the school performance of kids of color, girls and young women, and more recently, openly gay and lesbian students is crucially determined by their perception that mastery of school knowledge entails self-estrangement. Consequently, apart from the intrinsic educational value of a broadly based learning regime, one of the essential claims of some who advocate a large-scale effort to amend the established curriculum to include traditionally excluded cultures is that equality of opportunity cannot be fulfilled unless the student can see her/himself in the curriculum. The question before us is: Do students "fail" because the curriculum does not engage their perceived needs and interests?

The second trend has been in the relatively neglected area of pedagogy. Movements for educational reform at the local level aimed at arresting or reversing perceived school "failure" have gained new strength through Chicago's massive experiment in school-based management; New York's New Visions Schools initiative; and the spread of elementary education innovations such as "writing across the curriculum," decentralized classrooms, and curricular innovations that place new emphasis on teaching cultural and sexual difference.

The basic argument of the new pedagogy is that the classroom is the heart of the learning process. Following Paulo Freire and other pedagogic theorists, the prevailing conception of knowledge as a *bank* that stores valuables and dispenses capital to its borrowers is a primary cause of student turnoff (Freire, 1971). Contrawise, it is claimed, an *interactive* classroom that involves students in producing their own knowledge, and *mutatis mutandis*, their learning, may reverse the trend of large dropout rates among many city kids, especially from high school. We are still in the midst of this controversy.

Educational conservatives, which include a considerable chunk of modern liberals, insist that the multiculturals are imposing politically "correct" curricular criteria, whereas those who favor the curriculum of inclusion have insisted that the old universal curriculum favored dead, European men and excluded subordinated cultures (Schlesinger, 1992). Interestingly, education innovators include among their number some who would otherwise consider themselves free marketeers. For the hallmark of some curriculum reform is the goal of encouraging the individuality of the student by offering choices to replace the standard approach that places responsibility upon the school and the teacher to deliver a body of inherited knowledge for which students are then made accountable.

Whereas in the late 1960s and early 1970s the critique emanated from the left, it has passed decisively to the right. In recent years, it is the religious right and other conservatives who have most consistently interrogated the standard curriculum. In the wake of the fundamentalist attack against the exclusive focus of the biology curriculum on genetics and evolution, and conservative critiques of the alleged leftward drift of social studies textbooks—some have presented race, gender equality, and peace issues in a favorable light—liberals have found themselves, as in the abortion debate, in the stance of defenders of the status quo. Thus, the task of deconstructing and otherwise interrogating school knowledge from the left has fallen on hard times. Apart from the multicultural curriculum, the left has had almost nothing to say about the nature and the direction of school knowledge.

From the perspective of the school counselor, psychologist, or social worker, as well as a large segment of the administration, the task in city schools is to find the keys to "motivating" the learner to master the essentials of the curriculum. Most conventional educators who accept neither the contentions of various school reformers nor biological explanations for student failure such as race and its twin, intelligence, believe that given a relatively level playing field in purely educational terms, the problem of succeeding rests squarely on the learner. In this view, which remains the dominant one, the fundamental thesis of the conservatives that the culture of poverty—chiefly the absence among poor people of strong families and the work ethic—explains the inability of poor children to master school knowledge. Tacitly, this explanation has already linked school knowledge to a *style of life* associated with the job culture. It presupposes what needs to be explored: Are we still ensconced in the industrializing era that designates paid work as the marker of self-worth and social dignity? For if the job culture proves to have been a historically situated way of measuring value, then the ethical basis of contemporary life requires reexamination, and with it, the goals and purposes of schools.

After the distinctly social and economic orientation of the 1960s, during which educational performance was related to whether a kid and her or his family had a measure of economic security and freedom from relentless harassments of racism and sexism, the resurgence of individual psychology combined with a new version of the culture of poverty thesis to account for educational performance is surely distressing. But what unites proposals for reform that focus on curriculum, pedagogy, and school funding with individualism is the degree to which any of these positions takes the American dream as its starting point.

In the context of educational thought, the dream may be described as a tacit understanding that there are no long-term economic barriers to class mobility because the U.S. economy is sufficiently supple to weather all storms. Put bluntly, educational policy assumes long-term economic growth as a given.

Therefore the crucial issue is *opportunity* structure, of which access to education is a central component.[4] On this assumption, racism and other forms of discrimination, bad school organization, and archaic curriculum and pedagogy, and the unfortunate results of intergenerational poverty are seen as formidable obstacles preventing individual kids from doing well in school. But the proposal that the social structure of U.S. society is a zero-sum game is, simply, not entertained by educators, legislators, or indeed, almost anyone else except many high school students.

To account for the high, even alarming dropout rates among African American, Latino, Asian American, Italian American, and indeed most working-class youth, requires at least three kinds of analysis: historical, contemporary economic, and educational, that is, issues that bear on schooling itself as a discourse.

Historical Issues

Since the advent of compulsory public schooling and its enforcement by the turn of the 20th century, relatively few children of working-class families completed, or expected to complete, high school, much less go on to postsecondary schools. During the industrializing era of American capitalism, which spans the century after the Civil War, most working-class kids got working-class jobs in factories; in transportation; and after World War I, in manual, clerical, and sales jobs in retail and wholesale services. Many dropped out of school at the legal minimum age but were often considered delinquent well before then. With a factory job waiting, most teenagers could scarcely tolerate 8 years, let alone 12 years of schooling. Because all but the most skilled industrial work required little or no knowledge of reading, writing, and calculation, working-class kids—black and white—typically resented compulsory schooling because with the usual exceptions, they correctly perceived these years as a form of *detention* (Katz, 1971).

For these kids, schooling was a life chore one *endured*, but few expected to learn much, or indeed, to enter careers that might be opened up by acquiring cultural capital. Paul Willis's superb description of how working-class kids "fail" school in Great Britain obtains today for a very large segment of working-class kids of color and also many who are coded "white," especially those of Appalachian, southern European, and eastern European heritage (Willis, 1981). Willis's ethnographic investigation showed that what is coded as school "failure" is actually resistance by kids to the authority of school knowledge, the administration, and teachers. Although it is true that by rejecting the curriculum, kids condemn themselves to working-class existence, many view the price of rising above their class as too high for the promised rewards. Industrial labor may not always be pleasant, but until recently, it was fairly well paid, at least compared to many subprofessional jobs such as teaching, social work, and nursing and strong unions provided protection against arbitrary discharge and the unfair exercise of managerial prerogatives against labor.

More to the point, mastering school knowledge almost invariably entails leaving family and community; the world of relatives and close peer relationships must be surrendered, even renounced, in favor of the new world of professionalism. As a professional, the kid becomes a different kind of social individual; he or she must dress differently, consort with new people, and observe an entirely new set of rules. Few working-class girls were even afforded the option of escaping their fate of the double shift of housework and paid work. In contrast, for kids reared in middle-class homes, the transitions between family, school, and work are fairly seamless in an era when work defines the self. Moreover, strict parental upbringing and the "modern" family within the ranks of professionals and managers typically foster the autonomous development of the child; family resources also provide the basis for a wider range of choices at an earlier age than are available to working-class kids. Although school remains, for many, a ritual performance, as McLaren (1991) has forcefully argued, the student is prepared to endure its boredom and the rote learning entailed by the acquisition of cultural capital (Bourdieu & Passeron, 1977). For the goal of professional status helps the middle-class student endure the regimentation that marks everyday school life, regardless of how innovative the curriculum may be. The promise of becoming a doctor, lawyer, or computer programmer provides a rational basis for adapting to what may be perceived at the level of experience as knowledge abstracted from a kid's contemporary concerns. In short, for the middle-class kid, the experience of schooling may or may not be better than it is for working-class kids. What matters is: Schooling for what?

In the wake of urbanization and industrialization some school reformers sought to attract children of working-class backgrounds to school knowledge by measures that democratized the classroom, that is, provided spaces for kids to *participate* in the production of their own knowledge. John Dewey and his associates provided a theoretical framework for this strategy by insisting on the ineluctable link between cognition and practice (Dewey, 1916). It is not that Dewey argued that people "learn by doing"; rather his central claim was that practical concerns provide the context for theoretical reflection, because for him, theory was generalized practice. Dewey, George Herbert Mead, and later Harold Rugg, William Kilpatrick, and others developed curricula, advanced new pedagogic notions, and proposed a major shift in the architecture of the classroom to reflect a child-centered rather than teacher- or curriculum-centered learning environment. The object of all this was not to assist students to obtain the credentials necessary for professional and technical jobs; Dewey's aim was to transform public education into sites for citizenship, to prepare students to take possession of the political, if not the economic, system. For Dewey and his associates, keeping immigrant and migrant urban kids in schools had broad social aims, not vocational aims. In fact, it can be demonstrated that Dewey's concept of occupational education was that learning practical skills such as gardening were better routes than purely book learning to acquiring theoretical knowledge of biology. Contrary to popular myth, he did not advocate the vocationalization of schooling (Aronowitz & Giroux, 1985).

Of course, the fundamental function and the goals of schooling have been in contention for as long as education has been universal. Recall that many public school advocates, especially in the middle of the 19th century, preferred schools to child labor—or day prisons—to deal with the major problems attendant upon the gangs of children and teenagers who roamed and pillaged every important city and town.[5] In this mode, schools are conceived as *aging vats* when not constituted as training sites to provide the discipline required by the social order, including, but not limited to, the labor market. Others wanted a much more dedicated vocational curriculum for most working-class students. This objective is embodied in trade high schools, but also commercial tracks and the whole concept of "home" work, the imposition of a regimen according to which the school day extends from classroom to the home.

In the context of these debates, at the turn of the 20th century, Dewey's ideas were little short of revolutionary because his whole aim was to provide a positive philosophy and series of goals and strategies for school knowledge that addressed the problems of industrial society by reference to democratic, not market or juridical considerations. Schools would address social disorder by preparing students, whatever their occupation or socioeconomic station, to address the new problems of modernity: science and technology, mass culture, the massification of politics, and the consequent subversion of democratic processes. For Dewey, the labor movement, not schools, was the best vehicle to deal with the economic problems of working-class kids. The role of schools was to foster knowledge that could be fruitfully used in dealing with a panoply of life problems, of which work was only one. But the goal of education was certainly not identical with the specific needs of the labor market. Until well into the 1960s Dewey's ideas, although never dominant among educators, succeeded in creating a new vocabulary according to which the student was the normative subject of *education*.

Economic Issues

Two massive developments conspired to turn the attention of schools from some version of this social mission to becoming closely identified with labor market outcomes. The first was the GI Bill of Rights, which provided to literally millions of returning veterans the ability to complete high school and college, through substantial grants for tuition and living expenses. University and college administrations welcomed this development for a variety of reasons, among them the fact that through veterans benefits the federal government provided substantial aid to higher education. But the credentialing process, which in the last analysis remains the primary business of schooling, was given a big push by the concomitant expansion of public sector jobs, for which in many cases candidates were sorted on the basis of these credentials. The expansion of managerial, professional, and technical occupations in the private sector was also fueled by the tremendous growth in health and education services after the war.

After the war all kinds of paid work grew. From 60 million, the workforce expanded to more than 90 million people by 1970; the public sector expanded from 3 million jobs just before the war to 15 million in 1970, or about 15% of all jobs. In the midst of this exponential growth, factory employment rose only arithmetically from about 20 million at the war's end to 25 million by 1970. From 50% of the workforce, industrial and other blue-collar labor declined to about a third by 1970, and factory workers accounted for an ever smaller proportion of the labor force. Categories that were big winners were clerical workers, professionals, and technical workers. Many of the new entrants into the labor force were women.

During the war, hundreds of thousands of blacks and Latinos began to get well-paid factory jobs and many others were able to work in services outside domestic work for the first time. With farm work declining even as food production multiplied owing to incredible technological change, black sharecroppers and share tenants together with Latino farmers and farmworkers were thrown off the land and migrated to cities where they found work in factories loading on trucks, and blue-collar jobs in the public sector that in the great majority of cases did not require credentials of any kind. Even so, blacks finished high school in greater numbers, and, especially in the civil rights decade of the 1960s, gained access to universities.

Consider the New York area in the 1940s and 1950s. It was the world's garment center, with nearly 200,000 jobs in the men's and women's sections of the needle trades. It was the third largest machine tool and metal fabricating market and led in the production of pharmaceuticals and cosmetics. It was the biggest port in the country, a major trucking and rail center, and a leader in electrical and chemical manufacturing. Working-class kids, especially but not exclusively whites, had plenty of places to work after they graduated from or dropped out of high school. Similarly, Detroit was the world's car-producing capital. Chicago, in Carl Sandburg's words the hog butcher of the world, was also a leading center for manufacturing farm equipment, steel, and electrical goods and had considerable metals fabricating and men's clothing industries.

Certainly, many employers discriminated by refusing to hire black workers or relegating them to the lower paid and dirty jobs. And of course, in the building trades and skilled metal trades, such as tool and die, sheet metal, and others, blacks to this day have difficulty getting hired or obtaining apprenticeships. However, the period from 1940 to 1970 was marked by the entrance of literally millions of once-excluded African Americans into industrial plants, where abetted by union protections, they succeeded in building up considerable seniority and therefore job security.

The contemporary economic situation—"restructuring" and "deindustrialization"—has affected the entire country, but had particular significance in large cities like New York and Detroit where low- and intermediate-technology plants such as garments and metal fabricating have moved away or been forced out of business by, among other factors, international competition. In the 1980s the United States lost nearly 6 million factory jobs and another 2.5 million disappeared in the early 1990s. Capital flight has had a disastrous effect on all workers, but to the extent that it has wiped out unskilled and semiskilled jobs, black and Latino workers and their families and communities have suffered severe losses. For since the 1960s, the urban industrial labor force has been largely black and Latino. In the cities, the new jobs that were created in the wake of capital flight required bureaucratic or clerical skills, and in many cases, academic credentials. The 1970s and 1980s were a calamity for many young people, except the group that was able to obtain clerical jobs and entry-level technical jobs in the burgeoning financial services such as banking and brokerage, a boom that lasted less than a decade.

Compounding the economic shift was the fiscal crisis produced by the drying up of federal aid to cities and reduced tax revenues consequent upon capital flight and the low-wage service industries that replaced them. Today, high school leavers who would have entered these jobs—and for graduates, the tens of thousands of public sector jobs created between 1965 and 1980—have absolutely no employment prospects. The unemployment rate for workers ages 16 to 21 is 20%, nearly three times the national average. Only 15% of New York high school students have steady part-time employment during the school year, although more than 60% of them would gladly accept such jobs. And black and Latino unemployment for workers ages 21 to 35 remains over 40% in most large cities, including New York.

Even where the economy is relatively vital, such as in computer services and financial services, new jobs are not being created due to unencouraging economic forecasts. Employers prefer to pay overtime to existing workers rather than take on the burdens of added health, pension, and other costs associated with hiring new employees. Jobs for professional and technical categories are drying up as well as those for clerical and administrative workers. Moreover, in the past two decades, new technologies such as computers, fax, and photocopying machines have been widely introduced and have had an enormous impact on nearly all workplaces.

In colleges and universities, just as in public administrative
and corporate offices, which are relatively labor intensive, personal computers, voice mail, and answering machines are among
the technologies that eliminate many jobs, but not clerical functions. Now the professoriate and administrators assume most
of these tasks, and secretaries, file clerks, and receptionists are
not hired. And with the major reorganization of retail trades, a
change that resulted in the bankruptcy of Alexander's, the
sharp curtailment of Macy's branches, especially in suburban
shopping malls, and the closing of dozens of department stores
or branches of large chains, a major source of employment for
unskilled and semiskilled young people has been foreclosed.

There are still considerable shortages in nursing and some
technical categories of work in the health industry. But teaching
jobs at all levels are tight. Computer programmers are being
laid off as banks and brokerage houses merge, consolidate their
businesses into fewer locations, and introduce labor-saving technologies that eliminate technical labor. Unemployment among
attorneys and legal workers is beginning to erode this once-safe
profession. And computer-aided design and drafting has all but
eliminated the technical job of draftsperson, as engineers perform
this work with the help of the computer program, freed by three-
dimensional computer graphics to engage in the work of design.

In sum, there is little or no work in the above-ground economy and the kids know it. Among the sources of profound
paradox within the school systems of large urban centers is that
at a time when the links between education and work are
radically decoupled, administrators and educators are pressing
for a closer tie with business on the mistaken assumption that
the problems of student motivation could be greatly alleviated
if schools articulated themselves in every way with the labor
needs of major employers. As a result, there is a new drive
toward vocationalization, such as a renewed emphasis on co-op
education and revisions of the curriculum directed toward
courses that train students for specific occupations.

There are good reasons for initiating programs such as internships, apprenticeships, and the like. Students get a chance to

learn something about the world of work, and most important, get out of the stifling and confining environment of the class-room for a few hours a day or a week. But there is absolutely no evidence that beyond the small number of students who respond to innovative and exciting teachers and programs linked to traditional professions such as social work and teaching, occupational programs have significant effect in improving employment chances for the larger student population. Indeed, dropout rates are still very high. Many, if not most students, recognize that school knowledge has little or nothing to do with their lives, either present or future. For them, as well as for prior generations of children of the working and nonworking poor, a growing population in big cities, there is little or no point to buying into the curriculum, especially as the outcomes are more than indeterminate.

Educational Issues

In preliminary studies conducted by the Center for Cultural Studies at CUNY in high schools of majority African-American and Latino student populations, we found that most students who graduate from "at-risk" high schools—schools that have been designated by the board of education as those with low daily attendance and high dropout rates, lower than average academic achievement, and serious social and economic prob-lems—are from middle-class and stable working-class families (CUNY Center for Cultural Studies, 1993). Their parents work in the construction trades, own small businesses, or have steady, well-paying jobs in the health industry or education. These have been among the occupations that have survived budget cuts relatively well and resist industrial migration. More than three quarters of graduates from these schools go on to undergradu-ate schools, a proportion parallel to suburban high schools.

In short, school knowledge is perceived to be relevant, or at least tolerable, only by those students who have, in one degree or another, been formed in families with middle-class expecta-tions and the resources to support their kids. Educators can sometimes overcome the deep-seated economic and cultural expectations that students bring to schools, but cannot successfully motivate students who know, as most educators do not, that a high school diploma accumulates less cultural capital than ever before, unless it reflects a fairly rigorous academic course of study. To gain admission to most universities and colleges, students are required to demonstrate that they have met breadth requirements in science, math, and languages. Many city schools do not have adequate offerings in these subjects, indeed, do not have working laboratories or course offerings in languages other than English. But perhaps equally important, many bright students contrive to "fail" because they have rejected the implications of mastering school knowledge. Put succinctly, the street culture is their only community. It may be dangerous, but it offers friends, sometimes a way of making a living, and even some excitement.

So, school failure is preeminently a form of *resistance* to school knowledge, to class and other forms of social mobility. It is also an affirmation of the youth street counterculture that has once more become a subject of political and professional rumination. And what is striking and perhaps more distressing to mavens of social mobility for minorities and working-class white kids is that street culture has become increasingly attractive to students who would in previous years have readily entered the fast track. Students are aware that they must separate themselves from their peers in order to master the curriculum. This is neither new nor is it unexpected from the historical perspective. What is different is this: Rejecting the curriculum and other aspects of school authority no longer purchases entrance into working-class or many middle-class jobs. More to the point, kids are likely to remain unemployed or find "work" in various sectors of the underground economy—drugs; sex work (prostitution); or subminimum-wage production in garments, toys, and small electrical parts. Some turned toward the military until the recent budget and personnel cuts raised the qualification for admission into the armed services. The lack of a high school diploma is already a barrier for many who would otherwise find a life in the progressively shrinking armed forces. Within a decade, we may expect that the pared-down services may require postsecondary credentials as a prerequisite for enlistment.

A Proposal

The alternative to an even more frenzied attempt to make schools acceptable to businesses that have no room for school leavers is to reexamine the mission of schools. I suggest that educators ask whether schools can—or should—have anything to do with the job market. I believe schools should frankly be a place where the virtues of learning are extolled both for their own sake and also for the purpose of helping students become more active participants in the civic life of their neighborhoods, their cities, and the larger world. If these proposals sound utopian, they are—but only relative to the current myopic educational climate. If educators, parents, and kids are concerned at all with what has been termed "literacy," they need to note that all of the successful contemporary examples of countries that have achieved this goal are revolutionary, or at least radically, reformist societies. Despite profound economic and political differences, each of the following countries has achieved a level of literacy exceeding that of the United States: the now dissolved Soviet Union, Israel, Nicaragua, Cuba, Sweden, and China. Moreover, literacy among the perpetrators of the American Revolution was quite high: Most acquired their letters through an assiduous reading of the Bible, an activity that qualifies as ideological and even political in the context of the struggle for religious freedom in the 18th century. At their national inception, Israelis and Russians read Zionist and socialist and Communist literature, respectively, as a means to master language and achieve solidarity with the profound social changes that were under way. And Chinese children and adults poured over Mao's little red book on the road to acquiring the scientific, technical, and bureaucratic knowledge needed to build their society. These readings were, in various ways, linked to a

more or less clear vision of the good life, and in the cases of the
infant United States and Israel, of a democratic society.

Certainly, the good life embodied economic as much as social
and cultural elements. In these developing societies knowledge
was clearly fused with power over nature, over the hardships
associated with a new society, and over human adversaries, often
an interloper, an exploiter. Which is not to deny the degree to
which schooling in Communist and developing societies was
often obliged to purvey the ideological orthodoxies of the prevailing rulers. But even if democratic aspirations were cruelly betrayed
in many of these societies, education was closely linked to the
rhetoric of political, civic, and economic citizenship.

The problem with a scenario of radical education in the
context of the decline of ideological clarity in contemporary
politics is that none of the *alternatives* to professionalism, vocational education, and entrepreneurship—the troika of the current emphasis on education for jobs and business—seem cred-
ible. The movement for participatory democracy is in some
ways at a low ebb. Nevertheless, I have no doubt that even the
mild-sounding, but profoundly subversive demand for democratic participation as the goal of schooling is better than either
the ritualistic adherence to a curriculum that was outdated 25
years ago or the business-oriented educational reforms of the
current era.

Meanwhile, those of us involved in alternative schools, radical pedagogy, and the curriculum of inclusion could ponder
some aspects of our practice(s). For example, no high school can
be said to have broken with curriculum centeredness unless
students are involved in governance, including setting learning
goals, selecting courses, and having their own, autonomous
organizations, including a free press. Nor can the new schools
and programs ignore the imperative of citizenship, not limited
to the electoral system, but including discussions of social movements; a community-based curriculum in science and technology; and issues of class, race, sexuality, and gender.

For example, given that Brooklyn communities like Browns-
ville or Williamsburg-Greenpoint have some of the highest

pollution rates in New York and consequently high incidences of asthma, emphysema, and other respiratory diseases, the high school science program in these areas might initiate student-centered investigations of the nature and extent of and treatment programs for these diseases. In Ocean Hill-Brownsville, students might learn the history of the toxic waste dumping that has contributed to the high incidence of respiratory diseases among residents. In Williamsburg-Greenpoint, they might address the proposed building of an incinerator on the Brooklyn Navy Yard site, designed for garbage disposal. They would require basic knowledge of biology and physiology, interview and survey techniques, and use of health statistics and other sources of information. Moreover, they would have to learn how to use the library, not in a hypothetical way, but in order to do their project(s). They might decide to participate in the debate on the Navy Yard proposal.

Of course, what students would learn in the course of such investigations might get them interested in knowing more about science and even point them in an academic direction. But whether or not this outcome occurs, the exercise might foster civic engagement; they might learn how power works and how to confront it. And this may be the most important outcome of an innovative course of study, even if they remain in the community and do not take the path to professionalism right out of high school.

There is little sense of social and historical vision in the schools today. Neither the established authorities nor the reformers possess a way to describe the relationship between education and any possible challenge to the existing economic, social, and political order. At best—and only sporadically— some educational reforms articulate alternative cultural visions with reference to nationalism and populism, the twin pillars of identity politics. Although these efforts are surely necessary as a tool of engagement, they are by no means sufficient, because at the end of the day, the curriculum of inclusion refuses to address *class* issues. It cannot or will not speak to the contradiction between the now-surpassed elements of the largely middle-class American dream that undergirds the appeal to school knowledge and the legitimate demands that African Americans, Latinos, gays and lesbians, and other oppressed groups see *themselves* as subjects in the canon and the curriculum.

Notes

1. Chester Finn, now a professor of education at Vanderbilt University, was Assistant Secretary of Education for Research and Policy in the Bush administration, and during the late 1980s and early 1990s, voiced the proposition that throwing money at schools was not the answer to their problems, but instead advocated returning to a strong emphasis on the "basics" in school curricula as the most efficacious school policy. Because the Bush and Reagan administrations opposed federal aid to public schools in the belief that school funding was a local matter, Finn's influence was mainly ideological.

2. The Humanities and Arts endowments were established to provide federal financial support to artists, writers, and academics for a plurality of cultural and intellectual expressions. Congress's intent was explicitly opposed to government interference in the arts and scholarship. Although funds for these agencies were cut in the Reagan years, Bush, under pressure from his own right wing, managed to politicize these agencies to an unprecedented degree. For example, John Fromeyer was forced to resign from the Arts endowment, but only after denying grants to performance artist Karen Finley and others for their explicitly sexual politics. The Humanities chair Lynn Chaney openly proclaimed the agency's commitment to promoting only mainstream intellectual and cultural expressions. That the Bush era may not be quite over is demonstrated by the difficult time a Senate committee gave Sheldon Hackney, President Clinton's nominee for the Humanities endowment chair, during July 1993 hearings. Among his several moral misdemeanors, Hackney was accused of bowing to political correctness while president of the University of Pennsylvania.

3. The concept of "political correctness" may best be defined as the fear of being *perceived* as being racist, sexist, or homophobic. In its crudest form, to be politically correct means to restrict "hate" and other types of objectionable speech. However, its

historical roots lie elsewhere: It was used as an ironic term to describe some of the orthodoxies of the New Left of the late 1960s. Mockery has a way of becoming cant as the debates of the early 1990s amply show.

4. Perhaps the most influential treatise on the economic significance of education is Becker (1963). The accepted view that growth is an ineluctable feature of the U.S. and other advanced industrial economies is shared by liberal and conservative economists alike, indeed by the Marxist tradition as well. Economic crisis is regarded as cyclical, periodic, and occasional, and stagnation cannot be considered a permanent condition of capitalist economies.

5. Asbury (1929/1968) provides an extraordinary account of the extent to which Irish and other immigrant gangs, many of which were youth groups, engaged in organized vandalism throughout the 19th century. With Katz's (1971) account of school reform in the same period, one gains a radically different perspective on the rationale for public schools than that linking them to employment, or indeed, citizenship education.

References

Aronowitz, S., & Giroux, H. (1985). *Education under siege*. South Hadley: Bergin & Garvey.

Asbury, H. (1968). *The gangs of New York*. New York: Putnam. (Originally published in 1929)

Becker, G. (1963). *Human capital with a special reference to education*. Chicago: University of Chicago Press.

Bourdieu, P., & Passeron, J. P. (1977). *Reproduction in education, culture and society*. London: Sage.

Cremin, L. (1969). *The transformation of the school*. New York: Random House.

CUNY Center for Cultural Studies. (1993). *A student profile of five New York City high schools* (Report to the Council of Supervisors and Administrators and the United Way, New York).

Dewey, J. (1916). *Democracy and education*. New York: Macmillan.

Freire, P. (1971). *The pedagogy of the oppressed*. New York: Seabury.

Katz, M. (1971). *The irony of early school reform.* Chicago: University of Chicago Press.

Kristol, I. (1989, May). Comment on Francis Fukuyama's "End of history." *National Interest.*

McLaren, P. (1991). *Schooling as a ritual performance.* London: Routledge.

New York City Board of Education. (1992). *Annual report on Project Achieve.*

Schlesinger, A., Jr. (1992). *The disuniting of America.* New York: Basic Books.

Willis, P. (1981). *Learning to labor: How working class kids get working class jobs.* New York: Columbia University Press.

3. Talking Back: The Portrait of a Student Documentary on School Inequity

STEVEN GOODMAN

> Moving from silence into speech is for the oppressed, the colonized, the exploited, and those who stand and struggle side by side, a gesture of defiance that heals, that makes new life, and new growth possible. It is that act of speech, of "talking back" that is no mere gesture of empty words, that is the expression of moving from object to object, that is the liberated voice.
>
> *bell hooks (1990)*

In September 1992, our student-produced documentary exposing inequities in New York City public schools was broadcast on a Bill Moyers public television program. The shock waves it set in motion continue to reverberate in the lives of the students who made it and those who were its subjects, in the homes and

AUTHOR'S NOTE: I acknowledge with gratitude the generous support and assistance that I received from my wife, Suzanne Valenza, and my colleague David Murdock in composing this chapter and in the documentary work with students on which it is based. I am also very grateful to my colleague Bill Tally for the rich exchange of ideas about education, media, and the public sphere that he brought to this work.

schools where they live, and in the Bronx school district we portrayed. The narrative of the making of this documentary carries within it the story of how through the conscious act of creation, students make meaning of the world around them, and in turn, reshape themselves and their communities. The students' experiences and the community events that followed form a parable about the power of media education when harnessed to a liberatory pedagogy. In this chapter, I argue that media education has a central role to play in the revitalization of schooling as intellectually rigorous and democratic practice. I examine concrete experiences through the concepts developed by Dewey (1916; Fine, 1987; Freire, 1970; Habermas, 1989; Masterman, 1985; Mitchell, 1990; Wigginton, 1986) to attempt to illuminate media education as a means of transgressing the boundaries that separate school from community, artist from audience, thought from practice.

As educators teaching with and about the media, our pedagogy rests on some key concepts. We believe that the mass media have assumed a central role in the lives of our students and in framing the ways we think about our society. They work to forge a uniformity of values and public opinion. More than any other institution, they successfully cross the fault lines of race and class. Youth spend more time, on the average, watching television than in school. Television has become their master teacher. As students are increasingly exposed to mainstream media at home and in the classroom, media representations of social reality come to form their worldviews.

This need not be the case. Television audiences make meaning of what they watch through their interaction with the media; meaning is not produced by the media text alone. Although it is often an isolating activity (there is more than one television set in the average household), viewing can be an opportunity for active social exchange. Putting the power to create media in the hands of youth shifts the relations further from consuming culture to producing and reflecting on it. Media production in the classroom shifts the locus of learning from the teacher to the student. It provides an alternative model for learning where the social conditions of everyday life become the subjects of research and study. Documentary inquiries into community problems transform the master text from the state-mandated curriculum to the lived experiences of the students and their neighborhoods. Documenting conditions of exploitation is a form of bearing witness; connecting the individual to the system can transform oppressive experiences into liberating ones. Finally, putting the product of the media in the hands of the community through neighborhood screenings and discussions in a variety of forums builds an expanded public sphere. It creates an authentic public dialogue that transcends the moral and economic imperatives of the market culture.

The Narrative

Our student team spent almost a year researching, shooting, interviewing, and editing the documentary *Unequal Education: Failing Our Children* (Goodman, 1992) under the training and guidance of David Murdock and me at the Educational Video Center (EVC). What follows is a narrative of how these students set out to document the daily lives of two New York City middle school students in two very different schools and communities. The process of documentary broke the silence that had grown up around their own educational experiences. Through this narrative we will attempt to illuminate EVC's practice as intellectually rigorous and socially empowering, as providing a more profoundly meaningful educational experience for the student producers than was available to the younger students in either of the two schools they portrayed.

The method of documentary-based experiential learning requires a dynamic process whereby the students, with input from the instructor, constantly frame and reframe the purposes of their project. Over time, through the research, shooting, and editing processes, the students develop the voices and the craft to tell their story. Through their critical investigation of institutional practices, the students encounter both the periodic closing down of their inquiry and the inverse, the opening up of institutions to the media with false-positive public relations. This process leads to an evolving sense of the public sphere as questions arise about the limits of public dialogue and the power and limitations of television and of media divorced from television when viewed in an open public forum. In turn, questions about building democratic spaces for alternative cultural practices arise that counter the mainstream model of media production and consumption.

All four students who researched, shot, and edited the documentary were themselves products of the New York City public school system. Following Paulo Freire's (1970) "problem-posing" pedagogy, we posed the problem of their own educations. Although born in St. Thomas, Linden grew up in the Bronx and attended eight different schools before he graduated from Satellite Academy, an alternative high school at 21. While working on the documentary, he was a freshman at Hunter College. Carol's family came from Puerto Rico to the Lower East Side. She now lives with her mother in Williamsburg, Brooklyn, and is 20. Like Linden, she struggled through several different schools, eventually graduating from City-As-School, and is now at Hunter. Dawn, 18, was born and raised in the Bronx in a family of Irish and German background. She attended schools in the same district we documented. She has not started college. Carolie's family was from Neves in the Caribbean and she grew up in Central Harlem. At 17, she was the youngest member of the crew and was completing her senior year at Martin Luther King High School. Before forming the team they called YO-TV (Youth Organizers Television), the students had been trained in the EVC documentary workshop or in a school program affiliated with EVC. Now they were asked by Bill Moyers to produce, with his consultation and support, a documentary for his series "Listening to America." They worked on the project part time at EVC and were paid a stipend.

Once the team had decided to produce a documentary about education from the student's perspective, it was clear that the project would be very much rooted in their own experiences. Each of them was asked to examine his or her own school history. Out of their own narratives we created educational autobiographies.

Carolie, with her irrepressible smile and boundless energy, adjusted her glasses and told of her first memories, of how when she was in the first grade, her mother would watch her walk across an empty lot past junkies and winos all the way to the front door of her school. "In the seventh grade I got into fights every day, in class, in the lunchroom. Drugs were sold in and outside of the school. There were shootings every day. Then I got stabbed in my face by this girl. So my mother took me out of school." Reflecting on her past school experiences, Carolie felt that mostly what she learned, she learned from her mother.

It took some prodding to get Linden to share his story. Shifting his stocky body in his chair, he began,

> My first school was Holy Cross (the names of this school and the schools that follow have been changed). It was run by nuns. I was held back in the first grade. I remember the strict dress code. You had to wear a tie and name pin and I forgot to wear it every day. Every day. So the nuns made me stay after school for 2 hours every day and write on the blackboard: "I will not forget my tie." I hated to wear a tie. It was the clip-on kind, so it choked you when you buttoned your collar all tight. I got thrown out of school when me and my friends rang the door bell of the nuns' home and ran away.

He then went on to describe a string of eight different public schools he was transferred in and out of. Along the way, there were the familiar stories of fights, of cutting, of his growing sense of failure and disillusionment. After his mother found out that he had not been going to school for a year, he was admitted to Satellite Academy and finally graduated from there.

Carol took her journal out of her book bag and scanned her notes. Her brown hair fell around the shoulder straps of her denim overalls. She spoke slowly, almost in stream of consciousness, "There were fights every day. In the lunchroom, outside, after school, in the city buses. . . . One time I remember standing outside of school when a SWAT team invaded the housing projects across the street with their guns drawn. All the kids were just standing and watching. I remember being real scared of getting my sneakers stolen or my jacket or chains."

She was not admitted to the high school of her choice and ended up in her zoned school, which was overcrowded and poorly run. Its facilities were in a constant state of disrepair.

> There was no water in the bathroom sinks. They had rows and rows of lockers but they were barred shut so you had to carry your books and coat with you all day. They did this because of drugs. . . . I started hating the whole idea of high school. On the first day of 10th grade, a student was shot and killed in front of the school. I remember another time when someone was stabbed in the hallway and the blood was there all day. They started using electronic ID cards with holes in them when I was leaving, just like you were in jail.

Dawn pushed her hair away from her face, pulled nervously at her "Metallica" T-shirt, and told of her experiences,

> The third and fourth grade we had a real strict teacher. He hit us with a ruler and threatened us all the time. In the fourth grade we moved to a different room three times because more children joined the class. Then there were so many students, we moved to the gym. There were no desks or chairs there for a couple of weeks. In the fifth grade we also were in the gym. It was a big area with carpet on the floors taped down with that grey electrical tape. Other classes were in there too.

She was tracked into the above-average SP program in her junior high school. Drugs and fighting began to be a problem for the whole school. Her high school was overcrowded to the point that there were nearly 5,000 students in it.

Looking to the students for themes to explore through documentary inquiry is one of the fundamental elements of the EVC pedagogy. The central narratives of the projects are often the students' friends, neighbors, family members, and sometimes themselves. Our practice is supported by the research of Michelle

Fine (1987), who found pervasive silencing and marginalization of students, particularly students of color or low-income backgrounds, in New York City schools.

The writings of Paulo Freire (1970) also illuminate our methodology and the philosophy that guides it, particularly his concept of dialogue and praxis: "Dialogue is the encounter between men, mediated by the world, in order to name the world. . . . Once named the world in its turn reappears to the namers as a problem and requires of them a new naming. Men are not built in silence, but in word, in work, in action-reflection" (Freire, 1970, p. 76).

Our group's dialogue was in constant motion between the worlds of action and reflection. The students named their world through their recollections. They literally revisited their old schools as ethnographers, sitting in on classes, observing the process of education in action. They renamed their world as they moved beyond the self-referential to systemic recording of their observations in journals and reading Kozol's (1991) observations. After Carolie and Dawn visited Carolie's old junior high school, Carolie shared her observations with the group. She wrote of a seventh-grade art class that she visited where one student had transformed a brown cardboard box into a cemetery. In it, a tombstone read, "Mom, Louis and Papito RIP [Rest in Peace]. I love you and miss you." She learned that the family of the student who made it had died in a fire.

John Dewey (1938/1963) wrote, "There is, I think, no point in the philosophy of progressive education which is sounder than its emphasis upon the importance of the participation of the learner in the formation of the purposes which direct his activities in the learning process . . ." (p. 67). Following this principle, throughout the video production process, the students constantly framed and reframed the direction and parameters of their inquiry. From their collage of memories and observations they identified several emerging themes: the power of authorities and powerlessness of students, the chaos in the classroom and teachers' struggle for control, the segregation of poor students of color from middle-class white students, the impact of

parental and community support, and the pervasive violence in low-income schools and their surrounding communities. The team debated just how to tell this story through video, how to capture the day-to-day experiences of student life, deciding to focus on the experiences of seventh graders since they all agreed that was the time in their lives that they went through the greatest change. They agreed they should document the experiences of students from diverse backgrounds racially and economically. The students to be identified would be attending schools with very different student bodies, also reflecting economic and racial differences. This design would allow for any significant contrasts to emerge. The focal students would be equal academically; otherwise, the team cautioned we would be no better than the reporters on network television who constantly portray low-income minority youth as dropouts and failures. They chose District 10 as the site for the documentary, partially inspired by Kozol's work and partially because Dawn went to school there. Once the group made these decisions, new problems presented themselves, the most important of which was how to get access to the schools and students who would best bring to life the rich variety of themes they had identified.

Although we agreed this was to be a collaborative project in which the students would work actively to take all the necessary steps, we also recognized there was an important role for the teacher/group leader. I helped to provide the basic points of departure for their research. The students would take it from there, making calls, collecting information, and conducting interviews. Dewey (1938/1963) supports this notion when he writes,

> The principle that development of experience comes about through interaction means that education is essentially a social process. This quality is realized in the degree in which individuals form a community group. It is absurd to exclude the teacher from membership in the group. As the most mature member of the group he has a peculiar responsibility for the conduct of the interactions and inter-communications which are the very life of the group as a community. (p. 58)

Dewey's (1916) critique of schooling, written over 50 years ago, rings just as true today. He observed that most of what we learn in school is learned as fragments, separated from the actual experiences and conditions of life and carved up into one subject area or another. Such knowledge then can only be retrieved if the same compartmentalized teacher-centered classroom conditions under which it was acquired recur (pp. 47-48). In opposition to this, our approach to learning was more holistic and experiential. Whenever possible, we made sure that our students personally experienced the process of actively applying skills and strategies to the real-life problems they confronted in making their documentary.

For example, for the students to gain access to the schools they wanted to document, they had to write letters requesting information, interviews, and permission to videotape. It was an excellent writing exercise, but the point was, it was not just an exercise. It was for real; they had to write the letters to make their documentary. They corrected each other's writing and taught each other how to use the personal computer in the process. They ended up writing to several principals, and many of the letters took at least three drafts before they were good enough to send.

Within the documentary production process, my role and the role of my colleague, David Murdock, were constantly shifting. In some instances we were in the position of the teacher or group leader, at other times we were part of the group as coworkers. And sometimes, we were silent observers. Although the students corrected each other's writing, I was the one who set the standard of when the letter was ready to be sent. At other times, I was put in the role of the group spokesman, even though I was trying to be in the background and let the students speak for themselves. When we met with the first principal at Webb Intermediate School, Carolie began to explain who we were and what we wanted to do. But the principal and the assistant principal quickly grew impatient and wanted to hear from me. They wanted to get to the bottom line: Were we going to make a "positive" tape or a "negative" one? Then the conversation grew heavy with the weight of adult bureaucratic power. In the end, we got permission to visit the school, sit in on classes, and tape the average life of the students who go there.

At other times I slipped into the background. Visiting the school without cameras to search for an appropriate seventh grader to document, the YO-TV team clearly was in charge. The seventh graders immediately identified with the video crew, perhaps recognizing that these outside observers could have been their older brothers and sisters, and so were their allies who might bear witness to their plight.

Embarking on our first school visits, the crew assumed a heightened sense of observation. We all noted with great detail the school's physical environment and the social interaction within. Walking to the school from the subway stop we passed young crack-addicted prostitutes waiting in doorways. An abandoned lot was across the street on one side, bodegas lined the sidewalk of the front. The school must have been beautiful when it was built around the turn of the century, but now it suffered from water leakage that has damaged the structure and exposed the plaster on the inside. As the principal gave us a tour of the school, we came upon two fights in the span of about an hour and a half. In one case, the principal himself pulled a boy off a girl literally by his ear. We went into the library, but it was empty. Why? Because they don't have a librarian. The halls were generally busy with kids wandering around throughout the school day.

During our research visits to the school, we would split up and sit in on different classes to get to know the students and teachers. In one seventh-grade mid-level math class, the teacher tells us he is giving a test. He is a stocky young man who assumes a bit of the drill sergeant's attitude, but adds a sharp biting humor to put his charges in their places. Throughout the entire class period, the students are humiliated with an unending flow of verbal abuse.

Carol and Linden had been sitting in on another class. They find Dawn and me, and we try to decide whether or not to stay for another period or go back to EVC. We move down the hall toward the stairs. As we deliberate, a door flies open at the end of the hall nearest us and an African American boy is ejected from the classroom. The teacher struggles with the boy, trying to close the door, and the boy tries to get back in the room. He yells at the teacher, "Give me my hat! I'll bust you in the face. I want my hat!" We watch in amazement at this drama unfolding before our eyes. We watch as witnesses in case this should escalate into a violent incident. It does not. The boy loses and walks away.

We go off to get a bite to eat on Fordham Road and we all talk excitedly about what we observed. "My school wasn't this bad," says Carolie. "I can't believe this," says Linden. "They aren't learning anything! They are being cheated out of an education!" He is angry. He goes on to compare what he saw with what he read, "Well, it was really bad teaching, but I didn't see any overcrowded classes in the way Kozol described it. I mean everyone had a desk and a chair to sit in."

"But the building was old and run down. And none of the water fountains work," says Carol. "I checked them."

"How are we going to bring in cameras without totally disrupting everything? We need to catch things as they really are," I think out loud. "It's real different than the way the principal was trying to show us," Dawn observes. As it turns out, that was the problem.

When we traveled to the middle-class Riverdale neighborhood in the same school district to visit Woodhill Junior High School, the differences were striking. The neighborhood had a suburban feel of tree-lined streets with houses and cooperatives. Trees framed the school and a flag flapped in the breeze out front. The contrast of the school setting was immediately evident. Inside the school was clean and bright, with framed pictures lining the walls and student-painted murals on the lockers. The range of academic options and resources also contrasted with the school we had previously visited. There are three foreign languages taught there to the seventh graders: French, Spanish, and Hebrew. And students can take Regents-level earth science. The library was well stocked with 10,000 books. There were no fights and few students in the halls in between classes. A calmer feeling, more conducive to learning. A mix of white, Asian-American, Latino, and African-American students played outside in the courtyard during lunch. We never saw any white students in Webb Intermediate School, although there were a few Asian-American students, who we only saw in the enriched reading class. No students were allowed out of the building in the more impoverished Webb.

We prepared for our first day of shooting at Webb. We were following a class of mid-level tracked students. We followed them through their science, social studies, and English classes. The classes were chaotic, filled with tension, disruption, and frustration on all sides, but not really different from other days when we had visited without the camera. The camera could not help but capture this.

By the time we arrived back at EVC flushed with the excitement of our first shoot, the principal had already called and left an angry message for us. He wanted the tapes we shot and he wanted us to stop shooting. The project was off. He said he thought we were going to make a positive tape about his school and did not want to risk having our documentary destroy everything he had worked hard to build. We could not convince him that it was important for the public to know how the cuts in funding and resources affected the kind of education his students were getting and that it was important for the students' point of view to be heard. Once he discovered that we were talking to students and taping the disorder of the average classes, we had somehow crossed an imaginary line, transgressed a secret agreement that we would only tape positive things (he wanted us to tape the school chorus) and conspire with him to create an imaginary school through the magic of video.

The scenes we recorded were of alienated students walking in and out of the room during class, arguing with each other, talking back to teachers. These were acts of resistance to intolerable conditions in a public institution. We always knew this was sensitive stuff. Cameras in schools, especially cameras operated by students, make people with things to hide extremely nervous. The public's right to know what goes on in a public institution is often abridged by a veil of secrecy and silence. Bureaucratic control and ownership over the images and voices of daily student life are tightly held. And so we fast learned the lesson that the truth is defined by those who have the power to tell it. Evicting us from the school confirmed once again the institutional silencing of which Fine (1987) wrote. In this case, both the video team and the young voices they hoped to document and amplify were silenced. It was, apparently, too threatening.

The experience brought with it important lessons about the power of media and authority in schools. On one level it was profoundly demoralizing for the team. If the lesson of powerlessness and hopelessness was left uncontested, the project might have ended there. It reconfirmed feelings of failure and self-doubt. The challenge was to turn it into an opportunity that could enable us to see things more clearly and move forward. Through reflection on our actions and the reactions they caused, we came to see that in fact, despite his apparent power, the principal's fear of us revealed how vulnerable and impotent he really was in the face of the school system's overwhelming institutional power. This helped provide critical distance relocating the focus of the investigation from the individual to the systemic. Linden later recognized that as important as the principal of a school is, the problems of inequity in education could not be resolved by simply replacing a "bad" principal: "Of course I was disappointed about getting kicked out of Webb. But now that the project is done, maybe it wouldn't have been so good to show that footage. They would just blame it all on the principal."

We continued to visit Woodhill JHS and become more familiar with the students and teacher there while we searched for a second school to visit. Visits to several other schools and meetings with a series of parent activists finally led us to Bailey Intermediate School, located between the Grand Concourse and Webster Avenue in a black and Latino neighborhood plagued with massive unemployment, a thriving drug industry, and the constant threat of casual violence that accompanies them. Walking down the hill sloping to the school, it appears as a rather nondescript four-story orange brick building with bars on the windows and a flag in the concrete courtyard out front. Its architects won awards when it was built in the 1970s modeled on the "open classroom." No walls were constructed to separate the classes. Since then, walls have been erected, but often not all the way to the ceiling, so the sound from one class can easily be heard next door and in some cases far down the hallways. This construction makes surveillance difficult; the halls run diagonal to classrooms creating blind corners and little cul-de-sacs around the building's perimeter. Although cautious, the principal was supportive of our project and the learning process in which the video team was engaged. Once the superintendent gave us permission to videotape in schools, the principal gave us full cooperation.

A teacher introduced us to a group of his students whom he considered academically advanced. We requested this so that the students we documented here at Bailey would compare fairly to those we were profiling at Woodhill. The 13-year-old Lonnie stood out in the group. He was a slight boy whose sharp wit made up for his short size. We ended up focusing on him because he and his mother were both quite articulate, and unlike the case with some of his friends, both agreed to participate.

At Woodhill, after spending several weeks interviewing a group of students and their families, the material we shot pulled us in the direction of focusing on James. In a more perfect world, perhaps James and Lonnie could have been best friends. They are both handsome likable 13-year-old boys. Both were classified as "gifted and talented" students from an early age; Lonnie wants to be a lawyer when he grows up, and James wants to be a veterinarian. Both love to spend hours playing "Super Mario" and other video games, both were born and raised in the Bronx and suffered the death of their fathers. But James is white (of Jewish and Irish descent), lives in a private house in a middle-class tree-lined neighborhood of Riverdale, and attends a school with the reputation as a model for the district. It graduates more students to the elite Bronx High School of Science than any other middle school in the Bronx. It is ranked 25th in the city and has 65.9% of its students reading at grade level. Lonnie is African American (his family is from Martinique and Virginia), lives in a public housing project in a poor and violent section of the Bronx's South Fordham neighborhood, and attends a school that has a reputation as a school in trouble. It ranks 170th of city schools and has only 22.5% of its students reading at grade level. (A State Education Department monitoring team recently enacted a "School Under Registration Review" process there.)

Each school day in Riverdale begins with the pledge of allegiance and announcements from the principal. In South Fordham, the day begins with the principal walking the streets with walkie-talkie in hand, escorting his students to school safely. The resources available to the students in each school were not equally distributed, although the schools were in the same district. In James's school there was a full band, complete with clarinets, flutes, and trombones. Lonnie had to make do with Casio keyboards in music class. There was a microscope for almost every student in James's science class and a paraprofessional as well. Lonnie's class performed experiments without equipment. One day the teacher had them jump on and off their chairs as an experiment demonstrating how their heart beat and respiration would change. James spent afternoons and Friday nights playing basketball and other games at the community center located in his school. It was funded with local community support and staffed by the well-organized parents association (which also had the resources to award teachers with minigrants for special class projects). Lonnie spent hours at a time playing "Street Fighter" video games in the local pizza shop. Funding for after-school sports programs at his school had dried up and the parents association there was almost nonexistent.

The student documentary makers felt strongly that although the disparity of resources was important, this was not simply a story of material inequity. Observing student experiences in the two schools revealed something more complicated and less

tangible. What it came down to, what they found most disturbing in shuttling back and forth between the schools, was the
relative poverty of hope and spirit in Lonnie's school.

One cause of this was the flight of certified and experienced
teachers from South Fordham to Riverdale or the suburbs. This
left the least experienced teachers to struggle without much
support or training with the most daunting problems. Lonnie's
science teacher, for example, was not certified to teach science,
but had experience as a swim instructor and a dance and physical fitness teacher. As a second-year teacher, he was always on
edge and would routinely throw his feelings of frustration back
at the students in the form of ear-piercing screams that could
be heard far down the hall. Despite a small core of committed
and sympathetic teachers (Lonnie's English and law teachers
among them), the students' day-to-day existence was made up
of oppressive and dehumanizing experiences. We captured one
such experience as the science teacher, upset by the disruptive
behavior of his students, tried to start his class. He assumed a
martial stance with clenched fists at his side and screamed at
the top of his lungs, "Sit down now! Participate like human
beings today! Take out your textbooks! Take out your homework! And at least look like you can do some work!"

The intensity of witnessing such events evoked contradictory
feelings in the crew members: pride that they were bringing to
light the kind of abuse students routinely suffer and also fear
about what might happen as a result. Linden recalls, "I was
scared because I knew what we were getting was real stuff and
I knew teachers might get defensive. At times I didn't want to
point the camera at teachers because I didn't know what kind
of reaction they would have." Carol adds,

> When we kept bringing in the cameras in Bailey Intermediate
> School, I wasn't scared of documenting what I saw. I was scared
> of what people would take from it. Would they blame it all on the
> young people? Or on the neighborhood? Even though I knew I
> would edit it, I was worried that the wrong people would get
> blamed. I was afraid we would spread stereotypes of young peo-

ple as being uncontrollable. These are the stereotypes I always saw about young people on TV on the news.

As they reviewed their footage and began plan editing the material they shot, the students had lengthy discussions trying to sort out questions of stereotyping, representation, and who was really to blame. From what they experienced as students and what they observed as documentary makers, at first they concluded that the teachers were to blame.

Lonnie's mother, Liliane, recalls,

> Every night Lonnie would come home with a story. He would say the teacher told me, I'm not gonna make it, I won't be a lawyer, I'm not smart. . . . I couldn't believe it and the way the teacher would talk to me as a parent. One day I went there, he was cursing at the kids when I was right there. Then the kids would say, "You see, you see what I mean!"

In the students' hands, the camera recorded symbols of power, discipline, and surveillance that were pervasive in Lonnie's school. Things were out of control, and each day was a struggle to regain it. There was the real and ever-present danger that at any moment, a drug deal could go bad on the street outside the school and the students could get caught in a cross fire of bullets. Once safely inside the institution, the bars on the windows, the dimly lit halls, the guards (predominantly black and Latino), frustrated teachers (predominantly white), and whistle-blowing deans all communicated the sense of a detention center for juvenile offenders (whose offense, it seemed, was that they were poor, black, and Latino). Students were held in what was known as "captive lunch," prevented for their own safety from leaving the school grounds. The shrill voices of teachers demanding order and compliance could be heard in the halls. Control, not learning, was the name of the game.

The symbols of power and control present in James's Riverdale school were appropriately toned down, reflecting the community's greater affluence, stability, and security. There was no fear of drug dealers or shoot-outs on the way to school. Students were allowed to eat lunch outside in the local neighborhood. The halls were brighter, cleaner, more orderly. Discipline was often internalized here as self-discipline, in accord with the school's high expectations for student achievement. The teachers were also predominantly white, but the significant difference was this: The student body was whiter and economically better off than in Lonnie's school (about 25% were white in James's school, whereas we never saw a white student in Lonnie's school). Still, race and ethnicity were factors in James's school because there was stark evidence of tracking—the 65% black and Latino students were invariably in the lower tracked classes. Dawn observed, "In the classes, as the tracking went higher, there was more stuff on the walls, decorations, pictures, diagrams." But for James and his friends in the upper track, there was no question about the high hopes held for their futures. They were being groomed for the elite high schools (Bronx Science and Stuyvesant) and elite colleges.

Traveling between the schools and their communities as they did, the student producers could not help but gain a deeper understanding of how class and race shaped the contours of Lonnie and James's experiences. They came to learn that just because teachers were the closest and most visible authority figures to the students, they were not necessarily to blame. They came to understand the problems as broad and systemic.

By the late spring, Lonnie became so demoralized he was rethinking his career goal of becoming a lawyer, lowering his intellectual expectations. He tells us he changed his mind and now wants to be a basketball player. James has problems too. He does not make it to the honor roll and his mother feels that because of overcrowding at his school, James is not getting the kind of individualized attention he needs. But there is little doubt he will make it to college. James and his circle of friends have already identified their careers and the colleges they want to go: Harvard, Yale, and Columbia are among the colleges they plan to attend to become doctors, lawyers, and architects. James wants to go to the University of Pennsylvania and become a veterinarian because he likes animals.

On the last day of school James gets his report card and he finds that he passes all his classes. Lonnie and his mother meet with his guidance counselor to find out if he will make it to the eighth grade. Liliane explains that when she talks to his teachers, "They always tell me he's doing something wrong." When she presses Lonnie to explain why he always gets in trouble, he shrugs his shoulders and says softly, "They say I talk too much." He remains silent with a look of anger and disgust through the rest of the morning's meetings with counselors and teachers. Lonnie finds out that he narrowly escaped being left back. But he tells his mother that he refuses to attend the same school in September.

The day before school opened that September, the documentary was broadcast nationally on PBS. Bill Moyers then brought Jonathan Kozol and John Chubb on to debate the issue of school choice and vouchers. But the story didn't end with the broadcast, which rather signaled the beginning of a new phase in the project.

Lonnie's mother was outraged when she saw the tape on television. The conditions of Lonnie's school had been no secret to her. She had frequently sat in on Lonnie's classes, concerned about his progress. But it was the editing together of James and Lonnie's separate realities that made the difference. She had no idea what went on in schools scarcely 3 miles away in the white middle-class neighborhood. Seeing it all on television made the disparities somehow more real, more powerful, and perhaps more dangerous to her. She saw her son's science class, a room without any science equipment, filled with students jumping up and down on their chairs performing a "hands-on" experiment about blood circulation and heart rate. Juxtaposed to this she saw images of James's science class, a room full of students engaged in more meaningful "hands-on" experiments as they peered into their microscopes.

The community activists told us we were not saying anything new. Everyone knew the schools were unequal. It is just that we got inside and put it on tape. But the district board members and the administration of James's school were deeply upset. Although we were never directly addressed by any of our critics, we learned that we were accused of twisting and misrepresenting the truth. When a district school board member wanted to show the tape at a planning meeting, all of the other board members, except one, walked out. When it was not shown at a public board meeting, the dissident board member described the tape scene by scene to a packed auditorium of angry parents, children, and teachers. The rest of the board sat by in stony silence, not feeling the need to respond to questions about the distribution of money, resources, school safety, and staff development. In this case their silence was the silence of power, the power to prevent dialogue and to prevent action.

When asked if she was satisfied with the large audience she reached by the broadcast on public television, Carol responded,

> Even though it was on Channel 13, it's not as public as I would like it to be. Most of the people who came to the school board meeting, those parents wouldn't be watching Bill Moyers's "Listening to America" series because they have given up on the voting system to change their lives. The people we wanted to show it to were not seeing it. If the people at the meeting would have seen it, they could have gotten up and pushed the board aside.

Despite the fact that the tape was not shown, the open meeting became a forum, however limited, for the public to voice their outrage. The air was thick with the electricity of collective resistance and the potential for collective action, however fleeting. When a longtime African-American community activist got up to speak, he turned his back to the board in a potent gesture of defiance saying he had given up on the board and didn't want to waste his time even addressing them. The point was, if people wanted change, they had the power to make that change. It was simple. They had to vote out the board and vote in a new board. These board members should reflect the true diversity of the district (there were no African Americans on the board and only two Latinos despite the overwhelming majority of students of color in the district), but most important, they should be tireless advocates for their children. If they didn't vote, they had no one to blame but themselves. Once the so-called public part of the meeting ended, most of the audience left. In the lobby outside the auditorium parents flocked around us to request copies of the tape to show their neighbors. Inside, the board members went on with their agenda. Now they were in dialogue, but only among themselves, making the decisions that were the real business at hand.

Since that meeting, EVC staff and students have shown the documentary in a variety of public forums to spark discussion and galvanize support for better and more equal schools. Lonnie's mother held living room screenings and discussions for her neighbors. In addition, it has been screened at numerous schools, youth conferences, teachers workshops, and most recently at a conference on education law where the Bronx Legal Services decided to take up the issue of school equity and parent/student advocacy.

The making of the tape has had a profound impact on the young video makers. As Dawn noted,

> The process of making this project made me see my own experience differently. When you get a chance to see how things could be or shouldn't be, you're more aware. You see what else is out there. You see a teacher who does care, who does respond to the students. You see hallways with artwork of the students. It makes you feel better about yourself. When school doesn't have that it is much harder to get the students to cooperate. If the school is dimly lit, and has not been painted, what kind of positiveness will you get out of that? When you go into a school building there should be a feeling that makes you want to be there, that makes you want to learn.

For Carol, the project changed the direction of her career path,

> Now, I'm gonna be a teacher in a quote "undesirable" neighborhood. I was thinking about doing anthropology, the study of cultures, the study of cultures in New York City. I wanna be a video instructor, to teach young people to do video in their neighborhood and identify things in their neighborhood. . . . I have a lot

of questions. I want to start now. I don't want to wait till they certify me. I wouldn't be teaching science though.

Through our experience at EVC, we have seen that teaching students to document daily experiences of oppression and resistance, to bear witness, is a liberating pedagogy. Through the act of constructing a new reality on video, students learn a new way of seeing, expressing, and representing themselves. To paraphrase Dewey, they develop the capacity to look at the world as if it were otherwise. In the process of learning through documentary inquiry, a sense of community is reborn; through the process of organizing through community cultural work, delight in discovery and learning is rekindled. The public dialogues, whether in the form of street interviews or the public screenings, engage students, parents, teachers, and community leaders in collective action that is itself an affirmation of community and an expansion of the public sphere. It is a process that fundamentally emanates from a spirit of hope and resistance and from the courage it takes, as bell hooks (1990) put it, to talk back:

> The initial act of talking back outside the home was an empowering moment. It was the first of many acts of defiant speech that would make it possible for me to emerge as independent thinker and writer. Seen in retrospect, "talking back" became for me a rite of initiation, testing my courage, strengthening my commitment, preparing me for the days ahead. (p. 340)

We believe that there can perhaps be no more important educational project than to work side by side with students as they move from silence into speech, voicing resistance and hope for themselves, their schools, and their communities.

References

Dewey, J. (1916). *Democracy and education.* New York: Macmillan.
Dewey, J. (1963). *Experience and education.* New York: Collier. (Originally published in 1938)

Fine, M. (1987, February). Silencing in public schools. *Language Arts, 64*(2), 157-174.

Freire, P. (1970). *Pedagogy of the oppressed.* New York: Seabury.

Goodman, S. (Executive Producer). (1992). *Unequal education: Failing our children* [Videotape]. Broadcast on Bill Moyers's "Listening to America," Public Broadcasting Service, New York.

Habermas, J. (1989). *The structural transformation of the public sphere.* Cambridge: MIT Press.

hooks, b. (1990). Talking back. In R. Ferguson, M. Gever, T. T. Minh-ha, & C. West (Eds.), *Out there: Marginalization and contemporary cultures* (pp. 337-340). New York: New Museum of Contemporary Art.

Kozol, J. (1991). *Savage inequalities.* New York: Crown.

Masterman, L. (1985). *Teaching the media.* London: Comedia.

Mitchell, W. J. T. (Ed.). (1990). *Art and the public sphere.* Chicago: University of Chicago Press.

Wigginton, E. (1986). *Sometimes a shining moment: The Foxfire experience.* New York: Anchor/Doubleday.

4. Beyond Difference: Toward Inclusion and Equity

JOHN WOLFE

The enactment in 1975 of P.L. 94-142, the Education for All Handicapped Children Act, was a benchmark event in the long, often tortuous history of special education. Many years of lawsuits and legislative lobbying by parents culminated in this legislation that forced educators to examine the routine segregation of special education students. Though nowhere mentioned in P.L. 94-142, the concepts of mainstreaming, and later inclusion, emerged with the expectation that exceptional children would be educated in the least restrictive environment. P.L. 94-142 and subsequent related legislation inspired parents, students, and educators to ask a deceptively simple question: Which classroom setting—segregated, mainstreamed, or inclusive—best serves children with special needs?

The temptation to posit unitary and immutable answers for simple questions is great. Championing such solutions for education, however, is a prescription for failure. Humans are incalculably complex; the challenges of special education demand multiple answers as well as dynamic solutions. But educators are often quick to eschew the dynamic and mutable, preferring instead the pristine elegance of the self-satisfied: "Thus sects arise; schools of opinion. Each selects that set of conditions that appeal to it; and then erects them into a complete and independent truth, instead of treating them as a factor in a problem, needing adjustment" (Dewey, 1902/1959, p. 92). Awash in the ephemeras of education fashions, exceptional students continue to be victimized within rigid, unyielding systems perpetuated by those who erect "complete and independent" truths rather than confront the messy uncertainty of being.

This critical caveat—and the "deceptively simple" question underlying it—forms the scaffolding for this chapter, in which I outline varied definitions of mainstreaming, briefly chart the historical course of special education, discuss the tyranny of normalization, describe the movement toward inclusion, and propose choice for exceptional students as a way of breaking special education's cycle of failure.

Mainstreaming

What exactly *is* mainstreaming? Definitions abound: It has been called the instructional and social integration of special and regular education students (Kauffman, Gottlieb, Agard, & Kukic, 1975 [cited in Meisel, 1986]) and the integration of special and typical students in a single school where all children share identical resources and opportunities for learning on a full-time basis (Wang, 1981 [cited in Meisel, 1986]). Mainstreaming is the placement of handicapped children in regular classrooms for a portion of a day (Semmel, Gottlieb, & Robinson, 1979 [cited in Meisel, 1986]) and the phrase used to embody the least restrictive environment clause of P.L. 94-142 (Schulz, Carpenter, & Turnbull, 1991). Reynolds and Birch (1988) cite the rendering of special services to exceptional students attending regular classes. Biklen (1985), commenting on such varied definitions, concludes that mainstreaming has come to mean many things and cannot, therefore, be neatly defined, a thought echoed by Reynolds and Birch (1988): "In practice, mainstreaming means different things in different educational settings and can take many forms" (p. 20).

However they vary, most definitions describe the mingling of exceptional and typical children, a break with the bipolar pattern of education obtaining for most of this century, that is, regular and special education maintained as discrete and separate entities (Reynolds & Birch, 1988). Even though the history of U.S. education is peppered with isolated examples of integration, the term *mainstream* did not enter the educational vernacular until the 1970s and the passage of P.L. 94-142. This legislation and the accompanying push to integrate exceptional children into the mainstream reflected the influence of the civil rights movement and grew out of the Supreme Court's 1954 ruling (*Brown v. Topeka Board of Education*) that separate but equal was *inherently* unequal.

Beginning with the residential institutions of the mid-19th century, the course of special education in the United States has been a path through separate schools, segregated classes within regular schools, mainstreaming, and most recently, toward inclusion, unity, and the eventual effacing of all distinctions between regular and special education.

How have special education students fared? What outcomes have resulted from mainstreaming? Although early findings tended to emphasize success, Reynolds and Birch (1988) cite the lack of research involving control or comparison groups and the newness of the concept and conclude that "it is too early to answer questions about the relative outcomes of mainstreaming and other forms of special education with absolute certainty" (p. 21). Though P.L. 94-142 was a major impetus, the roots of mainstreaming predate the 1975 law, extending to a troubling concept, *normalization*, to which it is ineluctably linked.

Normalization and the Tyranny of Difference

Biklen (1985) writes that the term *normalization* was popularized in 1959 by Bank-Mikkelsen, a Dane. The term "characterized the policy of permitting people with disabilities opportunities to live in as normal a fashion as possible" (p. 6). Reynolds and Birch (1988) attribute the idea to another Scandinavian, Bengt Nirje, who believed that the mentally retarded should live in regular, normal, everyday environments.

Normalization, however humane and progressive its cast, is an idea wrought with contradictions. "Underlying the very idea of normalization," write Zigler and Hall (1986), "is a push toward homogeneity," which in a sense "can entail non-acceptance of an individual's difference" (p. 2). Normalization, and by extension mainstreaming, are processes by which individual differences are abraded. Assimilation of the handicapped or disabled "other" into the mainstream is the goal; the mainstream accommodates these differences while remaining essentially unchanged. This necessitates a continuing focus on exceptional students' "victim status and their problems as stigmatized persons, rather than assisting disabled persons in *redefining criteria by which success (or normality) is measured*" [italics added] (Phillips, 1992, p. 217).

Mainstreaming is therefore normative in orientation—making it, as will be seen, *very* different from inclusion. The special educator primes students, readying them for assimilation by the mainstream. In the vernacular of special and regular educator alike: "Andre is being mainstreamed for math and reading." Subtext: "Andre has been sufficiently *normalized* in cognition or behavior to be now acceptable for the mainstream."

Normative thinking is pernicious. If by definition some, but not all, children are "normal," what logically follows about the others is that they are *not* "normal" and must be otherwise characterized. They can be labeled exceptional, special, disabled, handicapped, retarded, physically or mentally challenged; such language bespeaks the need to classify and testifies to the terrifying poverty of our descriptive abilities. Further, these arch descriptors concretize the distinction between those whose presence defines the mainstream and all others. Normalcy becomes a mantle and a prize conferred upon the chosen few no longer deemed less-than-normal.

Dissatisfaction with normative thinking caused educators to reconceptualize the mainstream, suggesting that it ought by definition include the broadest possible spectrum of development. In this newly emerging definition, the mainstream is characterized, colored, and changed by *every* child. The *exclusive* mainstream, therefore, is oxymoronic: All children by virtue of being are normal and should be schooled together. The implications for students, parents, and educators were heady: Schools should be inclusive.

Toward Including All Children

Stainback and Stainback (1990) define the inclusive school as one where

> all students, including those who have been labeled severely and profoundly mentally and physically disabled, chronically disruptive, typical, gifted, or at risk are accepted, included as equal members, recognized for what they have to offer to the school community, and provided an appropriate educational program and any necessary supports needed for them to be successful learners. (p. xi)

Rejecting assimilation and integration, Stainback, Stainback, and Jackson (1992) note that those terms imply bringing someone *back* into the "mainstream of school and community life who had been excluded. The basic goal should be to not leave anyone out of the mainstream of school life in the first place, either educationally, physically, or socially" (p. 3). Schools, they note, are responsible for accommodating the needs of all students.

Inclusion fundamentally differs from mainstreaming in that no normative function obtains. A school is a community defined by all its students—typical, mildly disabled, gifted, multiply handicapped. Differences across the spectrum are neither effaced nor celebrated. They merely *exist;* they are realities.

Inclusion has administrative and programmatic implications as well. When all children are classed together, parallel administrative structures for regular and special education become redundant. And as the breadth of development in each classroom widens, teachers must encourage creative problem solving and develop ever-evolving teaching strategies for all students. Lockstep curricula and IEPs that merely catalogue "essential skills" will be instruments of failure. Adaptability and plasticity will have to become the norm.

Inclusive classrooms take different forms. Johnson (1991), describing Boston's Patrick O'Hearn School, asks:

> Which are the special needs children? Which adult is the special education teacher, which a "regular" teacher? It's hard to tell. . . . Two teachers team up to work with twenty students in each integrated class. They are often joined by other adults, such as an occupational therapist or curriculum specialist for integrating science and art instruction. (p. 45)

Tompkins Elementary School in the Croton-Harmon (New York) School District, in which no segregated, self-contained special education classes exist in kindergarten though third grades, offers a different model. Each special education teacher works with one grade and a single kindergarten class. Team meetings take place between 8:30 and 9:00 each morning. The special education teacher, no longer tethered to a self-contained classroom, acts as a consultant working in collaboration with regular education teachers, therapists, and other specialists. The special education teachers have set schedules that take them into each of their assigned classrooms daily; their work with the regular education teachers focuses on the entire classroom and not exclusively on the exceptional children.

Merricat's Castle School, a preschool nursery program on Manhattan's Upper East Side, is another exemplary model of inclusion. In its three classrooms, children with physical handicaps and terminal illnesses are schooled with typical children. Special and regular education teachers and an array of assistant teachers, aides, and student teachers work in each room. The effect is seamless: It is difficult to determine what is "regular" and what is "special" education.

The New York State Partnership for Statewide System Change, a project funded by the U. S. Department of Education, has 18 participating school districts, each committed to implementing quality, inclusive schooling for students with severe disabilities.

One cooperating district is the New York City Board of Education's District 75—the citywide school district providing services for children with multiple handicaps. There are seven New York City sites located in Brooklyn, Queens, Manhattan, and Staten Island.Programs at these sites vary in the extent and nature of inclusion. At P.S. 226 at 33, the Chelsea School in Manhattan, one aspect of the inclusion program involves five students with autism joining a slightly larger number of fourth graders for a weekly science class. In P.S. 811K at 329, in Brooklyn's Coney Island, six students are fully included in three inclusive classrooms, kindergarten and first and second grades.

Inclusive districts are being established all over the United States. The movement represents an attempt to forge a place for special education in the national educational reform movement—a movement from which it has been conspicuously absent. And like other elements of reform, inclusion is a response to the endemic, systemic failure of U.S. education.

An article in the newsletter of the Association for Persons with Severe Disabilities (TASH) comments on the National Association of State Boards of Education's (NASBE) recently released document, *Winners All: A Call for Inclusive Schools*, "Are children currently classified as 'special education students' achieving what they are capable of? Are they being prepared for life after school? Are current mainstreaming practices producing their intended outcomes? Is the separate special education system we have created the best way to educate these students? Has special education been asked to join general education in the reform movement that is now beginning to focus on standards, outcomes, and educating an increasingly diverse student body with individualized instruction? In responding to these questions, NASBE's Special Education Study Group has time and again been forced to answer, No!" (Mlawer & Falvey, 1993, pp. 1, 3).

The problem of negative outcomes in special education is well documented. Gartner and Lipsky (1987) write that "there is no compelling body of evidence that segregated special education programs have significant benefits for students. On the contrary, there is substantial and growing evidence that goes in the opposite direction" (p. 375). And Mithaug, Martin, Agran, and Rusch (1988), reviewing seven studies charting the transition of special education students (segregated and mainstreamed) from school to community life, conclude: "If we project the future of students enrolled in special education today, we would have to conclude that special education students . . . *will have received no measurable long term benefit from special education*" [italics added] (p. 16).

Given this record of systemic failure, will including exceptional students in regular classrooms prove any more successful than mainstreaming or segregation? Can the challenge of special education be fully met in the regular education classrooms of beleaguered school systems already plagued by failure or will inclusion become merely another catchphrase?

The inclusive school is but a vessel whose contents will help shape its success or failure. For inclusion to become more than a passing fancy, great care must be given to staffing, team-teaching approaches, and curricula that promote problem solving and creative learning strategies. Success will be measured by individual student outcomes. And what defines the *substance* of these individual outcomes? Expectations for students in *regular* education are implicitly understood: Schooling will lead to productive employment and independent living. The same expectations must also apply to special education students. But when measured against this relatively minimal standard, special education falls short. "Special education graduates fail to adjust after leaving school. They are under- or unemployed, earn subminimum wages, and depend upon their families economically and socially" (Mithaug et al., p. 22). Equity demands that all programs—regular and special—be judged by similar standards as to outcomes. Which setting—segregated, mainstreamed, or inclusive—proves best for children with special needs?

For some proponents, however, student outcomes alone are not the issue. For them, full inclusion has moral as well as pedagogical implications. Biklen (1985), citing as an example Lincoln's Emancipation Proclamation, suggests that inclusion is "not essentially a question for science. It is a moral question. It is a goal, indeed a value, we decide to pursue or reject on the basis of what we want our society to look like" (p. 3).

And referring to inclusion as "The Bigger Picture," an article in *Inclusion News*, the publication of the Toronto-based Centre for Integrated Education and Community begins: "Our key question as we initiate a new millennium is, 'How do we live with one another?' Inclusion is about learning to live WITH one another. Inclusion means 'being with'" (pp. 1, 2).

The evangelical thrust of such remarks suggests a perspective in which the needs of individual students may be subsumed in the name of "The Bigger Picture." Ascribing moral imperatives to programmatic decisions is disturbing if student outcomes become subservient to the goals of social engineering. For outcomes must remain primary. How else can program decisions be intelligently made? And how else can parents accurately assess a school?

Given the historical continuum, full inclusion is both inevitable and logical. But what assurances do students with exceptional needs and their families have that this latest turn in the special education road will prove any more successful than previous turns? What will prevent inclusion from becoming nothing more than the latest promising, but ultimately empty vessel?

Discourse in American education is too often cast categorically: whole language versus phonics, traditional versus alternative education, cognitive psychology versus behavioralism, self-contained special education versus full inclusion. Categorization trivializes debate, for implicit in its construction is a belief in singularly correct and finite responses to education's multiple challenges. Avoiding magical thinking—inclusion is *the* answer—is essential. But if neither inclusion, mainstreaming, nor self-contained special education are answers, what is left?

Toward Equity and Toward Choice

The national movement to reform and restructure public education has not included special education; *America 2000* says not a word about exceptional children. Choice is emerging as a keystone element in educational reform. Students (and their families) are seen as consumers increasingly able to choose from an array of educational sites. Magnet programs, schools-of-choice, schools-within-schools, and the problematic voucher system are designed in part to encourage students to shop around for the best school—a right families of means have always exercised.

But special education students operate within a closed set; for them, choice has never been an option. Professionals assess, evaluate, and place exceptional students. In the 1850s, placement meant institutionalization; in the 1950s, it meant segregated special education classes; by the late 1990s, it may well mean full inclusion. Whatever the setting, however, the mechanism remains the same: top-down, hierarchical decision making with professionals—"We know what is best for you!"—controlling the process.

Singular solutions imposed from above, even when well meaning and artfully crafted, cannot address the needs of every student. What is individually meaningful for a given student may be self-contained, segregated special education—think of deaf adolescents choosing to attend all-deaf high schools. For another student, it may be inclusive education or partial mainstreaming or some unique rendering of the two.

When special education students and their families can choose from a number of "special" options, equity will exist. Parents and students, given the option of choice, will decide which classroom best meets their needs. Not all parents in special education will choose "correctly"—neither will their regular education counterparts. But the subsequent give-and-take between professionals and families might help create a dynamic in which substantive change—born of professionals and families *listening* to one another—becomes possible. Sadly, however, choice does not exist for special education students, who unless politically savvy or wealthy rarely contest placement decisions. The new millennium will arrive when armed with the right to choose, special education students and their families weigh the cost-benefit ratios of inclusive, segregated, and mainstreamed schools and act on their choice. When special education students are conceded this basic right, they will become first-class citizens. But as long as its structure is inequitable—and as long as educators weld professionalism to infallibility—special education and failure will remain coterminous.

References

Biklen, D. (Ed.). (1985). *Achieving the complete school.* New York: Teachers College Press.

Dewey, John. (1959). The child and the curriculum. In M. Dworkin (Ed.), *Dewey on education* (pp. 91-111). New York: Teachers College Press. (Originally published in 1902)

Gartner, A., & Lipsky, D. (1987). Beyond special education: Toward a quality system for all students. *Harvard Educational Review, 57*(4), 367-395.

Centre for Integrated Education and Community. (1992). Inclusion—the bigger picture. *Inclusion News, 1, 2.*

Education for All Handicapped Children Act of 1975, 20 U.S.C. § 1400 et seq. (P.L. 94-142).

Johnson, E. (1991, Fall). We are all special: Inclusive education at Patrick O'Hearn School in Boston. *Equity and Choice,* pp. 45-47.

Meisel, C. (Ed.). (1986). *Mainstreaming handicapped children.* Hillsdale, NJ: Lawrence Erlbaum.

Mithaug, D., Martin, J., Agran, M., & Rusch, F. (1988). *Why special education graduates fail.* Colorado Springs, CO: Ascent.

Mlawer, M., & Falvey, M. (1993, February). NASBE calls for inclusive schools. *Newsletter TASH: The Association for Persons with Severe Handicaps,* pp. 1, 3.

Phillips, M. J. (1992). "Try harder": The experience of disability and the dilemma of normalization. In P. M. Ferguson, D. L. Ferguson, & S. J. Taylor (Eds.), *Interpreting disability* (pp. 213-227). New York: Teachers College Press.

Reynolds, M., & Birch, J. (1988). *Adaptive mainstreaming.* White Plains, NY: Longman.

Schulz, J., Carpenter, C., & Turnbull, A. (1991). *Mainstreaming exceptional students.* Needham Heights, MA: Allyn & Bacon.

Stainback, W., & Stainback, S. (Eds.). (1990). *Support networks for inclusive schooling*. Baltimore, MD: Paul H. Brookes.

Stainback, W., Stainback, S., & Jackson, H. (1992). Toward inclusive classrooms. In S. Stainback & W. Stainback (Eds.), *Curriculum considerations in inclusive classrooms* (pp. 3-18). Baltimore, MD: Paul H. Brookes.

U.S. Department of Education. (1991). *America 2000: An educational statement*. Washington, DC: Author.

Zigler, E., & Hall, N. (1986). Mainstreaming and the philosophy of normalization. In C. Meisel (Ed.), *Mainstreaming handicapped children* (pp. 2-14). Hillsdale, NJ: Lawrence Erlbaum.

5. Bilingual Education: A Double-Edged Sword in the Struggle for Equity

OLGA ROMERO

In 1970, the San Francisco Board of Education became the defendant in a class action suit filed on behalf of Kinney Lau and 1,789 other Chinese students. The children were failing in school because they did not understand English. The case was eventually brought to the U.S. Supreme Court (*Lau v. Nichols*, 1974), which sided with the plaintiffs with the momentous statement, "The problem will not be solved merely by providing students with the same facilities, textbooks, teachers, and curriculum; for students who do not understand English are effectively foreclosed from any meaningful education" (p. 563).

The Supreme Court, however, stopped short of specifying the form that these "alternative approaches" should take. In fact, Justice Douglas summarized the Court's position as follows: "Teaching English to the students of Chinese ancestry who do not speak the language is one choice. Giving instructions to this group in Chinese is another. There may be others" (*Lau v. Nichols*, 1974, p. 563).

As a result of the Supreme Court ruling, the "Lau Remedies" were adopted by the U.S. Commissioner of Education. These guidelines required school districts to identify and evaluate language-minority children and to create bilingual programs of instruction for those who did not know enough English to profit from mainstream education.

Proponents of bilingual education viewed the Lau Remedies as the opening for language-minority children to obtain equal access to public school education and a fair opportunity to succeed. However, most school districts around the country did not greet the Lau Remedies with open arms. The federal Office for Civil Rights set out to monitor district compliance and numerous lawsuits had to be settled before many districts reluctantly agreed to provide native-language instruction to students who did not speak English.

The fact that the manner in which bilingual education was to be put into practice was left up to the individual district's discretion did not help the cause of potentially bilingual children. Several models of bilingual education sprung up around the country, aiming to serve the needs of so called LEP children, or children of Limited English Proficiency. The different programs spanned a continuum from English as a Second Language (ESL) pull-out programs in which LEP children received ESL lessons several times a week to maintenance programs based on the notion that the child's native language ought to be developed and maintained throughout the child's schooling. In between, there were transitional programs offering instruction in the child's native language as well as in English only until the child had learned enough English to survive in a monolingual English classroom. Not all transitional programs were implemented in the same manner, however: "Early-exit" transitional programs measured success according to how fast the children moved to monolingual English classes. "Late-exit" transitional programs gave children more time in the native language to ensure literacy in that language. From its very onset, and in spite of the variety of ways in which it was implemented, the effectiveness of bilingual education was questioned by its detractors. In 1978 the American Institutes for Research (AIR) conducted a review of 38 bilingual programs and found no conclusive evidence regarding the value of bilingual education over the "sink-or-swim" approach in which children are immersed in the second language without regard for their native language skills. (Baker & deKanter, 1981). The AIR study received widespread criticism for its faulty design. Crawford (1989) summarizes the reaction to the study by the Center for Applied Linguistics as follows:

> Rather than testing an ideal instructional model, AIR . . . examined a patchwork of treatments labeled "bilingual" and had quantified their overall effects without attempting to control for a multitude of variables. Some reviews of the literature have adopted the same techniques: collecting evaluations, discarding those deemed unsound for methodological reasons, and essentially "counting the votes" for or against bilingual education. In such an analysis . . . the positive effects found with the good programs are often cancelled by the negative effects found with the bad programs. (pp. 87-88)

In the early 1980s, the Reagan administration commissioned a study ostensibly designed to provide an objective comparison between late-exit and early-exit transitional bilingual education. The study's final report, submitted by Aguirre International in 1988, contradicted prior research and actually provided data supporting the superiority of late-exit bilingual education programs over sink-or-swim immersion and early-exit transitional models. In view of the unexpected findings, the U.S. Department of Education contracted with the National Academy of Sciences (NAS) to convene a panel of experts to review the methodology and design of the study (Padilla, Fairchild, & Valadez, 1990). NAS approved the Aguirre methodology and the results were eventually released to the public in 1991 (Ramirez, Yuen, & Ramey, 1991).

Equity for Potentially Bilingual Children

According to the National Association of Bilingual Education (NABE, 1991) there are over 7.5 million school-age children in the United States for whom English is a second language. The U.S. Department of Education reported in 1992 that the population of students of Limited English Proficiency in the United States had increased by 14.3% since 1991. The figure they offered was 2,263,682 and this only represents students who have been "identified" by the school system. In other words, the figure could be even higher. It is predicted that by the year 2000, over 30% of all students in the country will come from families where the language of the home will not be English.

In spite of the fact that bilingual education had a difficult birth and continues to do battle with those who believe that "submersion in English," or the "sink-or-swim" approach, is the best way to teach language-minority students, it would be difficult to deny that bilingual education has made learning possible to many potentially bilingual children who would otherwise be denied access to an education.

In principle, all children who come to school speaking a language other than English have the right to be educated in an appropriate fashion so that they will be able to learn English and thus take full advantage of what our educational system has to offer. Unfortunately, bilingual education has been seen as a "compensatory" system of education. ESL pull-out programs and early-exit transitional programs are particularly viewed in this way because they present the bilingual program as a bridge that children have to cross before they can truly function in the mainstream. According to these models, successful children are those who are able to move out of the bilingual program in the shortest possible time. Children for whom the process takes longer are considered slow. Another red flag signaling the "compensatory" notion of bilingual education is evident in the very labels used to refer to children in bilingual programs. The label most commonly used to refer to children within the bilingual education system is LEP, or Limited English Proficiency. Potentially bilingual children are viewed as "limited" or "deficient" until they are able to speak English well enough to be placed in monolingual programs. Not surprisingly, the root of their deficiency turns out to be their primary language. In his report on bilingual education Crawford (1989) sums up the situation very aptly:

> Government changed the focus [of bilingual education] from an
> enrichment model aimed at developing fluency in two languages,
> to a remedial effort designed to help "disadvantaged" children
> overcome the "handicap" of not speaking English. From its outset,
> federal aid to bilingual education was regarded as a "poverty
> program," rather than an innovative approach to language in-
> struction. (p. 29)

The cognitive and social advantages of bilingualism (better
understanding of other cultures and groups and greater access
to job opportunities) have been virtually ignored by those who
see potential bilingualism as an obstacle for language-minority
children. In his review of the research on the cognitive advantages of bilingualism, Hakuta (1990) stated, "bilingualism can
lead to higher levels of metalinguistic awareness and cognitive
ability" (p. 58). Hakuta's own research confirmed prior findings by Peal and Lambert (1962), Diaz (1985), and others.

These advantages have not escaped the attention of more
affluent, mainstream parents. What Skutnabb-Kangas (1981)
has called "elite bilingualism" has always existed in the United
States. The children of privilege have traditionally been expected
to be at least bilingual. In her biography of Eleanor Roosevelt,
Weisen Cook (1993) talks about the beginning of Eleanor's education in England when she was only 15: "Entirely bilingual, Eleanor
was well prepared for the French-speaking school" (p.106). At the
school, Eleanor went on to learn German and Italian as well.

"Immigrant bilingualism," on the other hand, has not had the
same acceptance. Pedalino Porter, author of *Forked Tongue:
The Politics of Bilingual Education* (1990), argues: "Pushing home-
language maintenance bilingual education as a means of making disadvantaged, limited-English students 'balanced bilin-
guals' draws classroom time and resources away from the more
urgent educational needs of these children" (p. 207).

The difference in expectations could not be clearer. The advantages of bilingualism seem to be reserved for a fortunate
few. Not only that, but these advantages are casually turned
into disadvantages whenever the education of linguistic minorities is being discussed.

The goal of many a bilingual program (transitional early-exit programs in particular) has become to rid children of their undesirable first language as quickly as possible. The results of this kind of "educational surgery" are twofold: First, it causes what we know as "language attrition," a term used to refer to the loss of a language that has not been maintained or developed. Unfortunately, language attrition can often affect the level of proficiency that the child will be able to reach in the second language, because acquisition of literacy in the native language is the best predictor of success in the learning of a second language. That is, children who become literate in their first language have an easier time making the transition into second-language literacy than children who are not exposed to reading and writing in their first language. (Cummins, 1979, 1984). Second, the compensatory model of bilingual education causes children in bilingual programs to feel stigmatized. Many language-minority parents and their children believe that to be placed in a bilingual classroom is sign of failure on their part. When the short-term success of a program is measured by how quickly children abandon their native language, it is obvious that the linguistic base of the children's cultural heritage is being questioned. It could be inferred that the long-term success of these programs is measured by how well the cultural richness of these children is excised by the school. Thus the programs that were originally created to help are in many cases undermining the very children they were designed to serve.

Another problem faced by children in bilingual programs is the fact that they are often in classes segregated from the rest of the school or in schools that are made up totally of minority children. The situation has many root causes, including the ghettoizing of immigrants, who tend to congregate in specific areas and the flight of white middle-class students from urban public schools. Kozol (1991) presents a very clear picture of the gaps that can be found all over the country between rich, predominantly white school districts and poor, underfunded, predominantly minority school districts. What we see is either schools that are almost totally made up of language-minority children or schools where the bilingual program functions separately and is often in conflict (physically and philosophically) with the rest of the school. At this point it might be helpful to recap the Supreme Court's 1974 statement regarding the plight of many language-minority students: "The problem will not be solved merely by providing students with the same or at least comparable facilities, textbooks, teachers, and curriculum; for students who do not understand English are effectively foreclosed from any meaningful education" (*Lau v. Nichols*, 1974, p. 563).

The assumption made by the Supreme Court is that in addition to addressing the language mismatch, schools will provide language-minority children with the same facilities, textbooks, teachers, and curriculum. Unfortunately this is generally not the case. More common is the situation of immigrant children having to survive in extremely crowded classrooms and dilapidated school buildings where the textbooks that are used are inappropriate or there are no textbooks available, and the teachers from whom they receive instruction are the least experienced.

Within some schools, the label "bilingual" has become synonymous with underachievement. It is not uncommon for some bilingual parents to refuse to allow the school to place their children in the bilingual program for fear that their youngsters will not be able to reach their academic potential. In addition, bilingual programs are often called upon to deal with some of the most difficult problems faced by our schools, such as the high illiteracy rates found among new immigrant children of all ages (Lee, 1993), the arrival of new non-English-speaking students in the middle of the school year, and the education of migrant workers' children. In many schools bilingual classes and bilingual programs have literally become dumping grounds where any child who does not "fit the mainstream mold" is placed without regard for educational background or linguistic skills. Unfortunately, it is common to find "bilingual classrooms" in which some of the children speak no English at all and have had no schooling whatsoever; some have the rudiments of literacy in their native language, but do not speak English; some have rudimentary knowledge of English; and others are clearly dominant in English, having lost their skills in their first language. The teacher's job becomes to group children according to linguistic and academic ability and to provide grade-appropriate instruction to all of them. This practice of placing language-minority children haphazardly in a so-called bilingual classroom is probably the best formula for educational failure.

All of the problems already mentioned could be subsumed under the most insidious and difficult-to-fight situation faced by language-minority parents and their children: The "bilingual education facade," in which low-quality programs are set up and labeled bilingual, simply to placate the community, to comply "on paper" with district or board of education policies, or to prove that bilingual education does not work. In my job as an adviser I have visited dozens of schools in which potentially bilingual children are being educated. In general, bilingual classrooms are overcrowded, lacking in appropriate materials, and headed by the less experienced and less qualified teachers. We should always keep in mind that because of the many ideological disagreements by which it has been beset, bilingual education required a court order to implement and those who are not committed to the idea have used every available loop-hole to circumvent the law. For example, one of the mandates specifies that if the number of potentially bilingual children within a school is 20 or more, and if these children can be grouped into a classroom by age, the school has the obligation to hire a bilingual teacher to serve those children. It has been reported by several bilingual teachers and supervisors that when schools wish to avoid hiring bilingual personnel, they advise parents to transfer their children to other neighborhood schools so that no one school will have enough children to form a bilingual classroom. Parents are also advised (often by un-qualified personnel) to deny permission for their children to receive bilingual education, even when this form of education would be more beneficial to them. Bilingual evaluators also report that they are often pressured to recommend English as a Second Language programs instead of bilingual programs for handicapped children.

Equity for Bilingual Teachers

Bilingual programs have clearly provided a career option for bilingual individuals. In a sense, bilingual programs have created a market for bilingual teachers. Starting in the late 1960s, immigrants as well as language-minority students born and raised in the United States began to see teaching as their entrée into the U.S. middle class (much as their German, Irish, or Jewish counterparts did earlier in the century). The need to recruit bilingual teachers led to the creation of bilingual teaching programs in colleges and universities across the country. Federal (Title VII), state, and local funds were and continue to be appropriated for the preparation of bilingual teachers.

There is currently a high demand for bilingual teachers in most urban areas of the country. This unprecedented demand has also served to encourage members of linguistic minorities to join the teaching profession. However, it has also created many problems that affect both children and teachers. In large urban areas such as New York City, Chicago, Boston, Milwaukee, Newark, and Philadelphia, to name a few, hundreds of college graduates have been recruited to staff bilingual and bilingual special education classrooms. Although well meaning, these neophytes are often quite unprepared for the very demanding job of educating potentially bilingual children. In many cases these teachers lack the most essential teaching skills and even their language abilities are sometimes in question. The consequences to children in terms of equity are quite clear. As a result of well-intended policies, potentially bilingual children are being educated by some of the most inexperienced teachers within the system, and the situation is even more extreme within bilingual special education where diagnostic and intervention expertise is of the utmost importance (Cummins, 1984).

How are bilingual teachers themselves affected by this situation? Because many of them are not fully licensed, as they were brought into the system under "special circumstances," their jobs are in constant jeopardy. Also, because in some cases they replace monolingual teachers, the latter are resentful of the newcomers. Monolingual teachers, who may be more experienced and who may not even support the philosophy of bilingual education, feel that their livelihoods are being threatened by the new bilingual teachers. This competition has strained the relationship between bilingual and monolingual teachers. Even principals and other administrators, who have to comply with laws and regulations because of the language composition of their student bodies and who feel forced to hire bilingual personnel in favor of monolingual teachers, may not be totally supportive of their bilingual staff. Thus bilingual teachers are placed in a situation that appears as if designed to lead to failure.

Successful programs that encourage both Anglo and language-minority children to learn in English and in the language of the minority group are now serving as models of what a true bilingual enrichment program ought to be (Porter, 1990). Unfortunately, these dual-language programs are not widely known and so they become little enclaves where those in the know can and do place their children, but which are in fact off limits to most language-minority students. In many areas, the programs have to be modified because there are not enough Anglo children to create a linguistic balance in the classrooms. Thus dual-language programs are created in which all the children in the class belong to the linguistic minority and only the teacher can serve as a model for the two languages. These modified models, albeit not ideal, can also be successful if teachers, parents, and school administrators really commit themselves to language enrichment.

Conclusion

It is difficult, perhaps impossible, to separate bilingual education from politics. Unfortunately, few methodologies within education have been so clearly affected by the political tone of the times. The reasons for this connection are obvious: The history of public bilingual education in the United States started with the civil rights movement of the 1960s and it has been associated with poor immigrants and members of lower social strata.

Having been so far unable to separate politics from bilingual education, people's opinions about bilingual methodology are heavily loaded with conservative or liberal social views that may or may not relate to educational soundness.

It is not uncommon to hear people say "I don't believe in bilingual education" as if bilingual education were a cult or religion to which one adheres blindly. Bilingual education is a body of knowledge undergirded by a body of research. There are many myths surrounding bilingual education, to be sure. Pronouncements are made against it by people who have never taken the time to read the available research. People who might otherwise be perfectly rational and scientific minded throw all caution to the wind when it comes to offering opinions about bilingual education.

Those of us who believe that bilingual education is a form of progressive education to which all children are entitled have to join in an effort to develop a cohesive body of research, to disseminate successful programs, and to restore the real meaning of bilingualism. As with any other methodologies within education, bilingual education will only be as good as the people who carry it out. Enough funds should be allocated for the education of bilingual teachers. Emergency recruitment measures are not sufficient and can often be counterproductive. Programs need to be backed with enough supports to ensure the success of the recruits.

To destigmatize bilingual education, more dual-language immersion programs have to be created. When middle-class, mainstream parents understand the value of bilingualism and see it as a viable alternative for their children, two goals can be achieved: (a) better integration of Anglo and language-minority children within the schools and (b) public schools becoming more attractive to middle-class parents who might otherwise choose private school education for their children. This does not mean, however, that we should sit and wait for middle America to "approve" of bilingual education. Effective programs ought to be highlighted and replicated simply because they benefit language-minority children.

As long as bilingual education continues to be seen as something like an anti-American plot designed to thwart the homogenization of immigrants or what Schlesinger (1992) refers to as "the creation of a brand-new national identity, carried forward by individuals who, in forsaking old loyalties and joining to make new lives, melted away ethnic differences" (p. 13), it will be difficult for research studies and research findings to supplant righteous-sounding emotions and myths. As long as children who come to school speaking a language other than English are considered to be *limited*, there will be an overrepresentation of potentially bilingual children in special education classes, and both parents and children will fight the "bilingual" label. As long as a solid, comprehensive policy regarding the practice and methodology of bilingual education is not in place, we will continue to use a trial-and-error approach and to gamble with the future of our children.

As long as bilingual education is seen as a compensatory system of education reserved for the immigrants and the poor, any real equity considerations will be utopic. As long as bilingual education is viewed by the government and the public as the sole purview of language minorities it will continue to have stepchild status within the U.S. educational system. As long as there is no comprehensive plan to evaluate and place potentially bilingual children in differentiated settings according to their language background, experience, and literacy skills, bilingual classrooms will continue to be dumping grounds where only the very gifted will succeed in spite rather than because of the system.

Bilingual education could be a powerful weapon in the battle for equity among language minorities. As the number of speakers of languages other than English continues to grow and the U.S. population becomes more and more diverse, bilingual education has the capacity to prepare a large body of fully bilingual and biliterate individuals with enormous production and employment potential. It is unfortunate that such a positive force can and is literally being turned against the groups who could use it most.

References

Baker, K. A., & de Kanter, A. A. (1981). *Effectiveness of bilingual education: A review of the literature* (p. 8). Technical Analysis Report Series. Washington, DC: Department of Education, Office of Planning and Budget.

Crawford, J. (1989). *Bilingual education: History, politics, theory and practice.* Trenton, NJ: Crane.

Cummins, J. (1979). Linguistic interdependence and the educational development of bilingual children. *Review of Educational Research, 49,* 222-251.

Cummins, J. (1984). *Bilingualism and special education: Issues in assessment and pedagogy.* Clevedon, UK: Multilingual Matters.

Diaz, R. (1985). Bilingual cognitive development: Addressing three gaps in current research. *Child Development, 56,* 1376-1388.

Hakuta, K. (1990). Language and cognition in bilingual children. In A. Padilla, H. H. Fairfield, & C. M. Veladez (Eds.), *Bilingual education: Issues and strategies.* Newbury Park, CA: Sage.

Kozol, J. (1991). *Savage inequalities: Children in America's schools.* New York: HarperCollins.

Lau v. Nichols, 414 U.S. 563-572 (1974).

Lee, V. (1993). Low literacy immigrants pose new challenges. *New Voices, 3*(1), 2-7.

National Association of Bilingual Education. (1991). *NABE News, 14*(6), 1-3.

Padilla, A., Fairchild, H. H., & Valadez, C. M. (Eds.). (1990). *Bilingual education: Issues and strategies.* Newbury Park, CA: Sage.

Padilla, A., Fairchild, H. H., & Valadez, C. M. (Eds.). (1991). *Foreign language education: Issues and strategies.* Newbury Park, CA: Sage.

Peal, E., & Lambert, W. E. (1962). The relation of bilingualism to intelligence. *Psychological Monographs, 76*(546), 1-23.

Porter, R. P. (1990). *Forked tongue: The politics of bilingual education.* New York: Basic Books.

Ramirez, D., Yuen, S., & Ramey, D. (1991). *Final report: Longitudinal study of structured English immersion strategy, early-exit, and late-exit programs for language-minority children.* Washington, DC: Aguirre International.

Schlesinger, A., Jr. (1992). *The disuniting of America: Reflections on a multicultural society.* New York: Norton.

Skutnabb-Kangas, T. (1981). *Bilingualism or not: The education of minorities.* Clevedon, UK: Multilingual Matters.

U.S. Department of Education. (1992). *The condition of bilingual education in the nation: A report to the Congress and president.*

Wiesen Cook, B. (1993). *Eleanor Roosevelt.* New York: Penguin.

6. "I Will Have a Child in My Class With Two Moms, Two Lesbians. What Do You Know About This?"

ELAINE WICKENS
with
STEVEN SCHULTZ

Penny walked into my office in May 1989 and leaned against the wall. She told me that her principal just informed her that she would have a child with two moms in her public school kindergarten class and that she had better get ready for this. Penny was just finishing her first year of teaching. There was a moment of silence as she waited for my reply.

"Penny, I have never thought about this."

As a former teacher of young children now a faculty member guiding new teachers, as a curriculum developer, and as a political activist, how could I not have thought about the educational implications for families headed by two lesbians? As it turned out, this issue of children who have lesbian or gay parents had already been coming up in some graduate school classes and two other faculty members had been thinking along these lines. Others were thinking about this issue as well (Corbett, 1993; Patterson, 1992).

AUTHOR'S NOTE: A shorter version of this chapter was published in *Young Children, 48*(3), 25-28.

Penny's question led me to discussions with colleagues. We proceeded to design and enact our research. We interviewed those whose stories could inform—the gay or lesbian parents, the administrator, and the child's teacher. We wanted their experiences, their advice, and their questions to be available to others. Vivian Paley wrote, "There should be a sign above every classroom door that reads, 'All teachers who enter, be prepared to tell your story.' We teachers are more curious about the children than about ourselves, but seldom is there anyone around to question the questioner" (quoted in Ayers, 1989, p. vii).

We accepted this invitation to "question the questioner" and included the gay and lesbian parents and the administrators. We adhered to the triadic design when possible, excluding the teacher and administrator if the family had not come out (disclosed their sexual orientation and family structure) to the school. We also included two guidance counselors and three administrators unattached to a triad. The total population of over 30 informants are gay and lesbian parents and school staff who are white, African American, and Latino/a; middle class, working class, and poor. Their children attend private schools, day care centers, and public schools up through the second grade. We did not intend to include any children, but two children included themselves in the family interview and another child told the parents what they should be sure to tell us about her. For reasons of privacy, the informants' names have been changed.

We were also informed by the stories we were told at our presentations at national conferences, in college classes where we were asked to talk, by parent groups, and by our friends and colleagues. We interviewed families who had children ages 3 to 7. This is the period during which families enter the culture of the school. This rite—of special and sometimes traumatic importance for all families—presents gay and lesbian families with particular disclosure issues because most children will enter a school where the curriculum is in fact about the family. Stories about the family, books about the family, family members talking with the class about their work, home visits by teachers, and even class visits to homes are sometimes part of the family curriculum.

In any research, it is important to know the researchers' backgrounds: All of us are teachers of teachers, have taught young children and youth, have a background in research, and have developed educational materials. Two of us are parents, one of us is gay, one is straight, and one is a lesbian. Even though this is written by one person, it is impossible for me to write in the first person without hearing other voices, those of my coresearchers Steve Schultz and Virginia Casper, and of the people who informed us.

It's important to state some facts. There are 8 to 10 million children in 3 million gay and lesbian families in this country (American Bar Association, 1991). Some teachers will know that they have children coming from either gay or lesbian families in their class, most will probably not know. Still, lesbian and gay families are not a new family form. They have existed for hundreds of years (see Boswell, 1980, for a description of lesbian and gay parents during the Middle Ages in Europe; and Williams, 1986, for a description of gay men as parents in a number of Native-American cultures). What is new is a greater visibility of lesbian- and gay-headed families, a visibility that is in part due to a wider and louder social and political movement in the lesbian and gay communities and reflected in such recent publications by Martin (1993), Rafkin (1990), and Bozett (1987).

In considering Penny's question, we soon realized that she was asking about inclusion, about multicultural curricula in a broad sense. Inclusion is important whether there is a child with lesbian or gay parents in the class or not. The inclusion of diverse family structures and family patterns is even more complex when the family structure is not represented in the school.

How Do Teachers Know About Family Structure?

The way teachers learn about their children's families varies, ranging from home visits, conferences twice a year, a file card, a lengthy report prior to meeting a child, never reading records, or having any records. Some background is gathered in formal meetings and from conversations with other teachers and from other parents. Communication from the home to the school, and from the school to the home, is limited by time and is selective. Every family has issues of disclosure. For most lesbian and gay families, it is a central issue. Penny's story has a sequence that although not unique is rare. In this case, the lesbian parents talked with the principal, who talked with the teacher. The parents also talked with the teacher, who had a summer for planning.

Cathy, a young teacher at the beginning of her second year of teaching in a combined kindergarten/first grade in a public school, in reading through the file cards of her prospective children found one with "father" crossed out and "coparent" written in. Cathy said,

> Maggie and Ricky were written in. Even if Ricky could be either male or female, first thing that I thought of was that they were lesbians. Another teacher said, "How weird. Why would somebody cross out father?" She thought it was pretentious or something. And I said, "Maybe they are lesbian parents." And she said, "Oh, I didn't even think of that. That would make more sense." And so Lizzie [their child] was in the class for a week or something and I'd met Ricky. At one point Ricky said to me something about Lizzie's other mother. I don't know exactly how she phrased it but she said something about two mothers. And I said, "Oh, that's great." And she said, "It's really nice to speak to someone who isn't concerned about that."

Carla, an experienced early childhood teacher teaching 2- and 3-year-olds also read a card with "coparent." "In the beginning we almost didn't know whether they were sisters or cousins or whether they lived together, whether that was a permanent relationship or was it a temporary one. Were they friends? I guess if this is a permanent family we need to know that and is there a father?"

Jeffrey's parents had not yet come out to the school. Sasha, a teacher of 3- and 4-year-olds, asked if anyone did anything special over the weekend and Jeffrey said, "I slept in the big bed with Daddy and Matthew." Sasha said, "I wasn't even sure it was necessary to bring this up with the fathers. But it was a very awkward position, because I knew this about them and I didn't know what they thought I knew or what they thought I thought."

One mother who had not come out to the school and did not intend to was asked what she would like to do. She said if there would not be repercussions, "I would shout it at the top of my lungs, from the highest mountain. But that's not real."

All of these stories contain issues of disclosure—parents' wishes and fears, teachers' knowledge and bafflement. Disclosure, when not done in partnership, takes parents and educators only part way toward authentic communication. Just getting or giving the information is not enough. Parents and educators must figure out what to do with it as well.

When the family has come out, some principals inform the teachers, others prefer that the information be communicated from teacher to teacher. One guidance counselor discusses all families with the teachers. Some parents told us that the principal may tell one teacher and not another teacher. Other parents may assume that every teacher will know what coparent means. Two parents who had a child in a school that had student teachers wondered if the student teachers would be informed by the school or whether they would have to inform them.

It often takes time for a family to come out to the school. Jeffrey's dads had not come out to the school. Jeffrey was in one school from age 2 to age 4. Although his two dads had not come out to the school for 1 1/2 years, when they went to a new school, they came out before he began.

James, one of Jeffrey's dads, discussed how he felt about the different approaches he took at the two schools,

> Certainly there is a difference. Looking at how Jeffrey started Holland Elementary School and how he started the Brown School and not being open at Brown and having people do lots of guessing as opposed to being at Holland and being open, our relationships are very different. I think much more defined. Also, in terms of our own comfort, I think we're much more comfortable being out about this. [Names of schools have been changed.]

Matthew, Jeffrey's other dad, added, "It was a learning thing. The learning was that there is no choice but to bring it up. There's no way to hide it. Not that we were doing it so much on the conscious level." James added, "It's also giving a very negative message that what you're doing is wrong. So how can they have a clear, positive concept and understanding about what this relationship is about if someone's telling them not to tell anybody?"

But even though parents would prefer to come out, not all can. A parent who was a paraprofessional in a school close to her child's school knew if she discussed her sexual orientation with the school staff it would get back to the school she worked in and she would lose her job.

Context here becomes very important. Rather than a singular view of a gay parent's responsibilities about disclosure, educators may come to greater levels of understanding when they realize that many situations affect the freedom that each parent has to take the risk of coming out in a public sphere (Casper, Schultz, & Wickens, 1992).

So You Know You Are Going to Have a Child With Gay or Lesbian Parents in Your Class

One teacher made the decision to not teach her usual family curriculum. She just didn't know how to include gay or lesbian families. Another provided an atmosphere that permitted a 7-year-old boy to feel comfortable enough to refer to his two moms in class, but she did not refer to families with two moms or two dads when talking about diversity of families. When asked if she would read a book about a family that had two moms, a boy, and a dog and what they did during a week, she said, "I wouldn't without talking with all the parents because I don't want to teach about sex in second grade." We wondered if she would see herself teaching about sex if the story had been about a mother and a father, a boy, and a dog, whether there might have been more to her resistance than the fear of teaching about sex education.

Penny, informed through conversations with the two moms and reading materials they gave her, was ready to welcome a child who had two lesbian parents. All the children brought in photographs of their families and they were put up on the wall. They wrote and illustrated stories about their families; and in the hallway outside her room was a long mural with all the families represented.

Later that year, Jeremy was observed in the block corner with another child who asked him why he had two moms and no dad in his block building. He said, "I don't have a dad." The other child said, "You have to have a dad. How did you get started?" Jeremy replied, "My mom went to the doctor and got a seed and that is how I got started." These "natural" ways of including lesbian- and gay-headed families are very different from the fears of many opponents of the *Children of the Rainbow, First Grade* curriculum (New York City Board of Education, 1992) in New York City that this guide promotes the teaching of "sodomy" to young children.

Sasha, the teacher of 3-year-olds stated,

> It's like multiculturalism. . . . Last year was an interesting configuration because every family type existed, except for the two-mother family—single mother, single father, two fathers, everything. So it just sort of contributed to everything else we were dealing with in the room about who kids were.
>
> I did go on a real big search to find books about children and fathers, where there wasn't a mother included in the story. Which is not to say that I wouldn't have books in the room if there was a father and not a mother, but that was a very hard search. When, for instance, we read *The Runaway Bunny*, I sometimes talk about it as the father bunny instead of the mother bunny. And [the] kids will say . . . "Why are you saying father bunny?" And I'll say, "Because some people's fathers take care of them." That opened a real interesting discussion this year where I heard some child say, "Yeah, my daddy doesn't live with me, and sometimes I go to his house." And another child who has really been working this through sort of sat there with her mouth wide open, and said "My dad lives in Puerto Rico." So it really sort of freed everybody from wherever they were coming. If we sing songs, I'll change it to "Daddy" sometimes. So those are the kinds of things in terms of curriculum that I do.

One father came to me last year and said, "I just remembered, I grew up without a mother." His mother had died when he was an infant. "And I just remember Mother's Day was so hard when all the kids were making cards for their mothers." And I realized that within this school I think it's easier, not just because we don't celebrate holidays, but because of how we look at children. I don't think certain things would ever go on where you would just assume that everybody is from a family with a mother and a father and they're happy. Like from the 1950s.

Sasha's stories illustrate Dewey's idea that not only do unplanned learnings occur from experiences, but they are sometimes more powerful than the teacher's plan (Dewey, 1938/1963).

Questions and Assumptions

A teacher of 2-year-olds, who for the first time had a child in her classroom with lesbian parents said:

I think the most wonderful thing about the family we worked with was how open they were. I know I was apprehensive about it and it took time, as with anything. . . . I remember one of my first questions I had was about a book. It was called something like *Things I Like to Do With Daddy*, and I wasn't sure if I could put it on the shelf. It was just, well, why wouldn't I put it on the shelf? Ultimately, the thing was how do I address it when a child says, "I don't have a Daddy." Putting it in perspective, it could address a whole number of families . . . kinds of families. It would be the same kind of general questions, but specifically, it would be different in my mind. There was a level of newness to me about this situation. I had never thought about it before. That was significant too . . . that it had never occurred to me that this was a kind of family I would ever have.

Leslie, a teacher talking about a 3-year-old child to his lesbian parent said:

I remember when he was first at the center, and his fear of jumping off the [play] house. I remember just thinking, "Do you and Daisy get rough with him?" Where does this fear come from? I mean he is a tall lanky kid, you know, so [it could be that] just physically, he wasn't ready yet. But this is one of the things I thought, "If there were a man around in his life, that this would potentially be different."

Many teachers in the study had this kind of question: Would the child have a problem without a member of the family to act as a male or female role model? On the other hand, most parents did not have this concern. In fact, two moms wondered whether their son had been placed with a male teacher because they were lesbians. They did not think that this should have been the primary variable in his placement. In general, parents wanted their children to have adults in their lives who represented diverse cultures, careers, and sexual orientations. Along this line of thinking, two lesbian parents, one who was the biological mother and recently divorced, were glad that their son had a male teacher. And two dads made a conscious effort to have female baby-sitters. Some parents also thought of role models as providing humanistic behaviors that are consistent with their beliefs.

Implicit in teachers' discussion of gender role models were important questions: Would children raised in gay or lesbian families grow up to be gay or lesbian adults? Do girls need to have a male parent in order to recognize their own femininity? Do boys need a father in order to exhibit masculine behaviors? Do boys need to have a mother in order to recognize their own masculinity? These issues, which are dealt with in depth in other publications (Bem, 1983; Schultz, Casper, & Wickens, 1994) cannot be addressed fully here. Still, the raising of the questions to an explicit level is important.

Other teachers were worried about how their responses to children would affect their jobs. An experienced teacher of 4-year-olds heard one girl say to another girl, "When I grow up we can get married." A 4-year-old boy informed them that two girls cannot get married. Both the teacher and I overheard this. She turned to me and said, "I wish I could say to them that, yes, they could get married, but I know I would get fired." She asked me what I would say, and again, I had to say, "I never thought about this."

Since then, our research team has thought about it. We suggest that what teachers say will depend on the risk involved for the teacher. Risk is related in part to the community in which the school is situated and the school culture itself. Teachers also have different levels of comfort and experience in thinking about such questions. Possible responses might be:

"There are families that have two moms."
"You can raise a family together."
"Yes, they can."
"I have to think about it."

But better than answering their questions would be to ask the children what they know about families. And if they haven't heard about any families with two moms, adding, "Some families have two moms."

In lesbian-headed families, a question that often comes up is who is the biological, or "real" mother. Perhaps the family will inform the school about this. But advice from one couple was that teachers should make the assumption that the two mothers are involved in a committed relationship "and have an equal relationship to the child. If they [schools] would just make that presumption about gay families it would be tremendously helpful." As one 5-year-old child said to his moms, "You can't really get married in the law, but you're married in the heart. That's cause you love each other."

Sasha, the teacher of 3-year-olds, told a friend that she had a child in her group who had two dads, a gay-headed family. Her friend said, "Aren't you afraid of getting AIDS?" Sasha responded:

Most of the people I talk with who are not teachers have this reaction, shocking reaction, totally strange, they are threatened by it. . . . I was saying to this person who was shocked I was going over there for dinner, "I can see being very scared if you don't know. But I know this kid, and this kid sits on my lap." It has nothing to do with the AIDS question that he was bringing up, but I just know these people as people. They're not some arbitrary group that I just read about. This kid is in my life. He means a lot to me. I know this family.

In general teachers are examining their curriculum, modifying stories and songs to present parents of both sexes in protective and nurturing roles, and creating a climate where children can talk about their family structure, that they have two moms or two dads. The teachers, for the most part, are newly aware of this family structure. During the interviews, they found themselves thinking about their own personal beliefs, and we expect that they will continue to think about themselves, what they are teaching, and will develop both new strategies and new questions.

Sometimes both teachers and parents feel contextual limitations on their abilities to come out to the school or to create programs as inclusive as they would like. For example, the mother of a student of Saul's, a gay first-grade teacher in a public school, told him that she was a lesbian but didn't think she could come out to anyone else in the school. Saul also didn't think he could come out to the school. While all the teachers knew they had children of gay and lesbian parents, not all of them could teach an openly inclusive curriculum in their school.

Administrators

The climate of the school is created by families, teachers, the community, and importantly, the administrators. Penny was supported by her administrator and told to get ready. In our study, there was no administrator who would knowingly permit a child in his/her school to be hurt. The following quotes represent a range of acceptance of gay and lesbian families in their schools:

Director A: We are proud to have diverse families in our center, children with special needs, racially mixed families,

Principal B: children with two moms, children with two dads. I want to welcome you all.

Principal B: I am sensitive to all families: divorced families, families with single parents, gay and lesbian families. I'm sensitive to all families who have problems.

Principal C: I see this kind of family as disruptive to American life. I will not let books about this kind of family be read in my school. But no family or child in this school will be discriminated against.

Principal D: We have a very diverse population here, with all kinds of interesting differences from each other. We have physically disabled children, we have kids from shelters, we have kids whose parents have lots of money who took kids out of private schools to send them here. We have a very wide ethnic mix—Asians, Hispanic, Black, Tunisians, Yugoslavians. . . . Our teachers and our parents work very hard to preserve that diversity. I don't see that there would be any problem for a child with two mommies. So far as I know, that's been borne out.

These brief excerpts from the administrators' stories have the explicit and implicit message that no child will get hurt in their schools. Within their statements what being hurt can mean is open for examination. For instance, there are the potential hurting situations for a family headed by either gay or lesbian parents when their family is seen as one having problems. What will it mean if a child will never hear a story about his or her family structure?

What did it mean prior to the 1960s for children—all children—to have basal readers where Dick and Jane, mother and dad, dog named Spot, white family, lived in a white house? Some children in the 1960s did have basal readers that included children with brown faces, families with brown faces, called integrated readers. Now there are many fine books for children and youth where cultural, ethnic, and social diversity are woven into the themes. Today there are a number of children's books where the parents are gay or lesbian. (See Chapman's, 1992, annotated bibliography). One principal who did not know of these books asked me to check if there were any of these books in his school library and to ask the librarian to order them if they weren't there. I asked if they should be in classrooms. He said, "That would be up to the teacher."

Where I went to high school in West Virginia in the 1940s, I never heard a teacher use the word "Negro." I heard the word "Jew" in my senior year when we read *The Merchant of Venice*. What is it like for a child to never hear the words "gay" or "lesbian" spoken by a teacher or administrator? What does it do to the image of a family when the principal includes children of gay and lesbian parents in the category of "those with problems"?

Children Sharing—Teachers Sharing

Recalling Paley's wish for teachers to give voice to their stories (Ayers, 1989), we think that we can learn from what children and teachers share with us about their lives. For example, Lizzie, age 5, told her teacher, Cathy, that she wanted to tell her something. Cathy told us:

Well, she told me the other day that she would tell me something, but she wanted to tell me privately. And I said, "Okay." There's a couch in my room that sort of serves as a private conversation place. And so we sat down, and I said, "What is this about?" And then she got really silly, and she kept saying that she was embarrassed, and then she said it had something to do with sex. She said, "And I know I'm not supposed to talk about that, because it's private." And I said, "Well, this is a private conversation. If you want to tell me about it, that's okay." And she told me, "There's mommy kisses and there's daddy kisses, and there's different kinds of kisses." And all she gets is mommy kisses. She doesn't get daddy kisses. And I said, "Well, how are daddy kisses different?" And she said, "Men have scratchy chins and stuff from having hair on their face." And I said, "Do you have uncles or anything?" And she said, "Yeah, I have a bunch of uncles." And I said, "Don't you get kisses from them?" And she said, "Yes." Then I said, "Then you're getting kisses that are sort of like daddy kisses." And then asked her if there was anything else. And she was like, "No." I think she's thinking that she's missing out on something, and she doesn't know yet that in a lot of ways she isn't. I don't think she is. She has two very supportive, wonderful parents, and other supportive adults in her life as well.

Sasha, teacher of 3-year-olds:

This is just a very funny anecdote. At this age [when children hear] Jeffrey say "I have two dads," it doesn't have a whole lot of meaning for them in terms of what his family is about. So one day when his baby-sitter came to pick him up, [Abe] said, "Jeffrey, your mom's here." And he said, "That's not my mom, that's my baby-sitter," and added, "I've got two daddies." And the kid he was talking to looked at me, looked at Jeffrey, looked back at me, like checking this out. I said, "You know, he does. He has two daddies." And quickly [Abe] turned to Jeffrey and said, "I've got two daddies too." (laughter) And you could see him working it out. The next day I was waiting with Lenny, another boy. We were waiting for his father, who usually picks him up, and there was another man coming down the hall. And Abe said to me, "Oh look, it's Lenny's daddy." And it clearly wasn't Lenny's daddy. "That's not Lenny's daddy," [I said.] And Abe said, "Yeah, that's Lenny's other daddy." Abe will go home and say, "Where's my other daddy?"

We developed a book about a family with two moms, a boy, and a dog. Penny read it in her class. After reading it she asked the children what they liked about the book.

Donna:	It is nice, it has a birthday in it.
Pete:	I like it because it is nice and has a birthday in it.
Sarah:	Because it has a lot of nice stuff in it, it has a birthday.
Alice:	It is nice to have two moms.
Max:	Just like Jeremy.
Penny (teacher):	Why would you like to have two moms?
Alice:	Because no one else would have two moms. And you're the only one who has two moms.
Doug:	Jeremy does.
George:	I have two moms.

Penny
(teacher):   George, you have two moms? One in Korea, one here?

George: One in Korea, she died.

As researchers with a point of view, we were most pleased that a book would elicit, "It is nice to have two moms." And then George reminds us that there is really not much that you do that is done only for one child. George had never talked about his mom in Korea.

Penny told me, "I hope when these kids get older and some-one says a homophobic thing that they will say, 'That's not true, I know Jeremy.'"

Saul, a first-grade teacher:

> It would be easier if the words gay and lesbian were accepted words in children's vocabularies like the word Black is a part of these kids' vocabulary. I'm afraid to use those words in a first-grade classroom. I'm already under attack all the time because I teach whole language reading, because I'm a first-year teacher who's really not doing very well, because layoffs are coming, because teaching in the public schools is not a supportive atmosphere, period. So using the words gay and lesbian in the classroom would really be the straw that broke the camel's back. And that's really scary. And no amount of awareness or consciousness on my part can change that. I don't know how to approach that dilemma.

Saul continued,

> One piece of advice I'd have for any teacher, of course, is to never tolerate any kind of homophobia in the classroom, or this sort of 6-year-old prehomophobia that I see. A child called me faggot on two different occasions, when he was angry, and he gets angry at me when I scold him. And this year, because I'm so overwhelmed, I have a short fuse and I'm not always as even tempered as I need to be with the kids. And both times, there was enough chaos in the classroom that I couldn't sit down and deal with the issue the way I wanted to. But I wanted to send a very clear message that this kind of language is not tolerated in the classroom.

Now there was a third incident soon after this, and it hasn't happened since—this is all in a very short period of time—when he called another child faggot and the kids went "Whoooo," 'cause they already figured out that I don't allow that word. I turned and asked, "What does that mean?" and another child at the table who is very macho looked at me and said. "It means punk." And I said, "What's a punk?" And he said, "It's a homo." At this point he's completely exasperated by my stupidity, but I still asked him. "What's a homo?" And he said, "Someone who can't fight."

James and Matthew told this story about their son, Jeffrey: "At the supermarket checkout the cashier asked Jeffrey where his mother was. Five-year-old Jeffrey answered, 'I don't have a mom. I have two dads. These are my two dads and I have a friend who has two moms.' 'Oh,' she replies and bags the groceries."

There will be many more wonderful stories from teachers, children and families. We hope they will be told and will help us all understand a family structure once unfamiliar.

Wishes

We hope the words gay and lesbian will become easy words in our vocabulary. What would it be like, when talking about families, to say, "Today in our town some children live with a mom and dad. Some live with grandparents, some children live with lesbian parents—two moms—some children live with gay parents—two dads. There are many different kinds of families; families with one mom, one dad; some children live with foster parents. Can you think of any family I have left out?"

This might be even more important in a community where no one ever has had the opportunity to hear a child pridefully say, "I have two dads and I know a friend who has two moms." Yes, we hope the words gay and lesbian will be easy words in our vocabulary.

Conclusion

I grew up in West Virginia and attended segregated schools through high school. When I went home in the 1950s, about a year after the schools had integrated, I saw children of different colors pushing each other on swings, riding their bikes together. It is a small town—population about 3,000—has six streets, a train that divides the town down the middle, a river, and is in a valley with mountains on each side. It is a town where people will call to you and invite you to sit on their porch and talk. When I came home, I was able to talk with teachers who had taught me in both elementary and high school. It was easy during our porch talk to ask, "How come things seem to be working so well?" Each teacher in one way or another said, "Because we knew it was going to happen and we didn't want any child to get hurt." It would be simplistic to say that all lived happily ever after. But to ignore the explicit intent of educators to make a difference and include all families into their school curriculum would be to deny optimism.

In our research, in one way or another, "that no child will get hurt" is what the educators were saying to us. But it is also true of these teachers and administrators that some were able to create an inclusive curriculum and others could not. Some parents felt able to come out to the school and some would not. Disclosure by parents and invitations from school faculty are so important in making teams that work for the child in school and at home. Martin (1993) advises parents, "As difficult as it may be to do, in the long run it is easier for us and our children if we can approach the school personnel directly and explain the family to them" (p. 324).

Even with the ongoing current attacks against inclusive curricula with books with stories about families that have two moms and two dads; even though teachers in some instances will still lose their jobs if they respond in the affirmative to a child's question, "Can a girl marry another girl?" it is no longer a secret that there are teachers like Penny who want to have their questions answered. There are a lot of other people who are working to make it possible for "inclusion" to include families headed by gay and lesbian parents, and I, who was awakened by Penny's question, now have thought about it and will continue to do so.

References

American Bar Association. (1991, August 25). ABA annual meeting provides forum for family law experts. *Fam. L. Rep. (BNA), 13,* 1542, 1543.

Ayers, B. (1989). *The good preschool teacher.* New York: Teachers College Press.

Bem, S. (1983). Gender schema theory and its implications for child development: Raising gender-aschematic children in a gender-schematic society. *Signs: Journal of Women in Culture and Society, 8*(4), 298-616.

Boswell, J. (1980). *Christianity, social tolerance, and homosexuality: Gay people in Western Europe from the beginning of the Christian era to the fourteenth century.* Chicago: University of Chicago Press.

Bozett, F. (Ed.). (1987). *Gay and lesbian parents.* New York: Praeger.

Casper, V., Schultz, S., & Wickens, E. (1992). Breaking the silences: Lesbian and gay parents and the schools. *Teachers College Record, 94*(1), 109-137.

Chapman, S. (1992). *The power of children's literature: A rationale for using books on gay- and lesbian-headed families and an annotated bibliography.* Unpublished master's thesis, Bank Street College of Education, New York.

Corbett, S. (1993). A complicated bias. *Young Children, 48*(3), 29-31.

Dewey, J. (1963). *Experience and education.* New York: Collier. (Originally published in 1938)

Martin, A. (1993). *The lesbian and gay parenting handbook: Creating and raising our families.* New York: HarperCollins.

New York City Board of Education. (1992). *Children of the rainbow, First grade.* New York: Author.

Patterson, C. J. (1992). Children of lesbian and gay parents. *Child Development, 63*(5), 1025-1042.

Rafkin, L. (Ed.). (1990). *Different mothers: Sons and daughters of lesbians talk about their lives.* Pittsburgh and San Francisco: Cleis Press.

Schultz, S., Casper, V., & Wickens, E. (1994). *Tentative trust: Enhancing communication between gay and lesbian parents and the schools.* Unpublished manuscript, Bank Street College of Education, New York.

Wickens, E. (1993). Penny's question: "I will have a child in my class with two moms, two lesbians. What do you know about this?" *Young Children, 48*(3), 25-28.

Williams, W. L. (1986). *The spirit and the flesh: Sexual diversity in American Indian culture.* Boston: Beacon.

7. Striving for Equity in Mathematics Education

BARBARA DUBITSKY
with
PHYLLIS EILENFELDT
LINDA METNETSKY
MICHELLE MORALES

The social and political consequences of mathematical illiteracy provide alarming signals for the survival of democracy in America. Because mathematics holds the key to leadership in our information-based society, the widening gap between those who are mathematically literate and those who are not coincides, to a frightening degree, with racial and economic categories.

(National Research Council [NRC],
1989, p. 14)

Mathematics is becoming an increasingly important tool for effective citizenship and for productive work. Yet it has been an accepted fact, well documented in the literature; increasingly in recent years (Hsia, 1988; NRC, 1989; Rock, Estrom, Goertz, & Plooack, 1986), that mathematics is largely the province of white males and Asian Americans, both male and female. The mathematics education community is increasingly coming to see this situation as intolerable and projecting pathways for change (Apple, 1992; Commission on Standards for School Mathematics, 1989; Commission on Teaching Standards for School Mathematics, 1991; NRC, 1989).

In this chapter we review issues of mathematics and equity and describe our attempts at Bank Street College to support change in school mathematics teaching. In the second part of the chapter, we analyze the change process through the words of three graduate students engaged in the process.

Mathematics Teaching and Equity

Mathematics has traditionally been an important component in fields such as the physical sciences, architecture, and finance, but now mathematics and mathematical thinking are becoming increasingly important in the biological and social sciences and even in such fields as nursing, law, and nursery school teaching. The traditional mathematics sequence of arithmetic, algebra, geometry, and calculus classes constitutes only a fraction of the mathematics people use in their careers:

> Challenging problems in such diverse fields as computer science and social science have invigorated the discipline of discrete mathematics, a field that reflects both computer logic and human ambivalence. Moreover, new mathematical tools such as game theory and decision theory are being applied to the human sciences where one seeks to make choices, decisions, and coalitions on some rational and systematic basis. (NRC, 1989, p. 5)

However, one must recognize the limits of who might achieve the mathematics knowledge required.

> Many young adults of color and from low socio-economic backgrounds are being excluded from their chosen fields because they have not learned to think mathematically not only in professional fields but also in blue collar jobs. For example, machinists who once moved tools by hand, now, through computers, must manipulate them with mathematical symbols and reliance on

trigonometry and coordinate geometry. (Martin & Scribner, 1991, p. 598)

Further, too many citizens lack the mathematical tools and confidence to use them to be intelligent about such current problems as the national deficit, fairness in tax structure, protection of the environment, efficient ways to prevent crime, and equitable school financing. Many children, especially those from lower socioeconomic levels, are most often taught mathematics algorithms by rote. Among the contributing factors to this phenomenon are that parents, teachers, and administrators expect and demand less of children as their social class decreases. Teachers of children of lower socioeconomic status often themselves have not had the same educational opportunities as the teachers of children of higher social classes, and teachers lower their expectations as to the probable occupational futures of children as their social class decreases (Anyon, 1980). With fewer opportunities to solve problems and to gain the basic conceptual understandings necessary for continuing their mathematics learning many children from low socioeconomic groups cannot gain entry into a wide variety of occupations.

The Curriculum and Evaluation Standards (*Standards*) issued by the NTCM (1989) outlined a new way of conceiving mathematics education, seeking to change mathematics teaching from arithmetical, algebraic, and geometry skills and facts to be memorized and used in solving routine "school problems" to a rich array of mathematical topics including data collection and analysis, probability, statistics, and such topics ranging from discrete mathematics as graph theory to theory of elections, and principles of fairness. The NTCM *Standards* encourage the use of applications while learning mathematics and the learning of mathematics in an atmosphere where children are encouraged to communicate with each other both in oral and in written forms. The *Standards* encourage the availability of learning with modern tools, calculators, computers, and other manipulative devices to aid in problem solving. A salient feature is the idea that to know mathematics, one must do mathematics. Concomitantly, assessment is seen as an ongoing process in the classroom that includes teacher observations, project work, portfolios, and tests that employ calculators and computers and nontraditional problems, as well as more traditional pencil-and-paper tests. The overall goal is to help students understand the value of mathematics in their everyday lives; to help them become more self-confident learners; and to increase their ability to solve problems, to communicate mathematical notions, and to reason mathematically.

A critical issue that we educators face is which children will experience the excitement of the kind of learning that will meet these goals. Our past record in engaging poor and working-class children in higher cognitive reasoning activities is not strong. Anyon's (1980) study of five schools, three in a medium-sized city and the other two in a nearby suburb, composed of students from different socioeconomic backgrounds, illustrates critical class differences in curriculum. In the working-class schools, children were learning all subjects by rote, using mechanical procedures. These students had no choices, they made no decisions; there were no opportunities to express their thinking. Further, material was often taught in fragments with no explanations about why the children were learning them. In the middle-class school the basic goal was for children to get right answers by following correct procedures among choices presented. The teachers recognized cognitive processes to some extent as they asked children to explain how they got their answers. They did not, however, ask children for creative solutions or thinking. In the affluent professional school, children were asked to be creative, to work independently, to use real-world problem-solving situations. Although this school did not stress communication and cooperative work among students, in other ways their outlook on teaching mathematics in the late 1970s was much the same as that called for in the NTCM *Standards*. In the executive elite school children were encouraged to analyze their work, to make decisions, to challenge solutions of other children. These children were seen as the possessors of correct answers, not the book or the teacher.

My observation of schools in New York City reflects today the same class differentiation in curriculum. In schools with mostly poor children, the teaching emphasizes rote learning; by contrast in schools where more of the families of children are affluent, the children are asked to make their own decisions and come up with their own solutions for solving mathematical problems.

Bank Street's Response to
Differentiated Teaching of Mathematics

How can class-differentiated teaching change? Without strong mathematical backgrounds and analytic skills, many teachers do not know how to teach in any way other than the traditional. (Silver, 1992). Teachers need considerable outside intervention to change their understanding of what mathematics is and how to teach it. This is particularly true of teachers of poor children who haven't questioned the limitations inherent in traditional practices.

Like others trying to create change, we at Bank Street designed the Mathematics Leadership Program to enable teachers interested in mathematics to become model teachers of mathematics and school mathematics leaders. More recently, a National Science Foundation grant allowed us to create the Mathematics Leadership Collaboration, a collaboration between Bank Street College and 10 New York City public schools. The program consists of coursework, advisement in the field, and collaboration as the participants take leadership roles to enable their schools to change the nature of curriculum, practice, and inclusion for girls and minority children. The schools we are collaborating with all have populations that are largely African American or Latino. The teacher/leaders have become leaders of mathematics leadership teams in their schools, which are working, with guidance from faculty, to improve the mathematics teaching in their classrooms and to consider the needs of the diverse populations in their schools. Faculty advisers are helping them observe the nature of mathematics learning and to shift from didactic and rote approaches to approaches that allow children to construct their own knowledge. These teachers are learning to have different expectations for their students' achievement as they observe the level of mathematics they are capable of creating.

The Program and Participants' Experiences

The Mathematics Leadership Program addresses the issue of teachers needing a deeper understanding of the nature and scope of mathematics by teaching them a wide variety of mathematical topics, many from emerging mathematical fields. They learn this mathematics in the same way we want them to teach children and other teachers: They construct their own knowledge using materials that model the mathematical essences of problems from the real world. The curriculum relies heavily on the precepts of the NCTM (1989) *Curriculum and Evaluation Standards for School Mathematics* discussed above. We help these teachers take on a leadership role in their school through coursework and in an ongoing seminar called Practicum in Leadership.

Laura, Monica, and Pamela discuss their experiences in the programs and their classroom practices. Laura teaches middle school mathematics in a racially and economically integrated private school in Brooklyn, New York. Monica is a kindergarten teacher in Harlem. The African-American children she teaches come from very diverse backgrounds, some from families that have lived in New York City for generations and others recent immigrants from other parts of the United States, from islands in the Caribbean Basin, and from Africa; many are poor. Pamela teaches at the Young Adult Learning Academy (YALA), a school for high school dropouts run by the Department of Employment. The students are African Americans and Latinos ages 17 to 23, 50% of whom are parents. They attend YALA for 4 months and then are placed in jobs. They go to math, reading, and writing classes each day for an hour and must complete a portfolio in each subject area. They are working toward a GED.

Laura enrolled in the Mathematics Leadership Program in order to confront unfair stereotyping about girls and math. She also wanted to learn more about the middle school math program, specifically the use of manipulatives. Monica believed the program would enable her to become more proficient in math and thereby a better teacher. For Pamela, the teacher at YALA, gender issues were also important, linked with cooperative learning techniques. Laura, Monica and Pamela discuss the changes that have taken place in their classroom teaching. Laura has had experiences with female students in her 6th-, 7th-, and 8th-grade classrooms that illustrate the importance of students working cooperatively with each other and the use of social content in mathematical activities as discussed by Fox (1976). She reports:

> I kept looking at how to structure a learning situation with manipulatives that allowed the learner to construct his/her own knowledge. I began to talk to other adults about their math experiences—what made math work for them. Could they explain the math that came easy? When did math become difficult? Did a person affect their thoughts about math? Several women told me that they never understood anything about math. . . .
>
> One girl, Sarah, comes to mind. I first worked with her in the sixth grade. She was an avid reader but not at all interested in mathematics. Sarah became hooked on mathematics as she was asked to solve problems in cooperative groups. The visual stimulation of the manipulative materials along with the discussions and the writing that the groups did about the problems they were solving involved her and the other girls in her class. In eighth grade she would spend hours of her free time building and solving quadratic equations with Cuisenaire rods. She and the other students in her class worked together making up complex equations in order to play the computer game Green Globs. Now in eleventh grade she is a superior mathematics student (and so are several of the other girls she worked with).

Important factors concerning girls' achievement in mathematics are its perceived usefulness (Fennema & Meyer, 1989;

Meyer & Koeler, 1990) and "sex role congruency" wherein a girl may have the "perception that others see her as somewhat less feminine when she achieves in mathematics" (Meyer & Koehler, 1990, p. 63). Laura is aware of these problems when teaching girls at the middle school level:

> I also realized that middle school students bring to the learning situation a distinctive mixture of early childhood and adulthood. Tied in with the learning of mathematics are the issues of developing egos, of self-esteem, of trying to balance social concerns and realities with academic demands. Girls want to be liked and popular, often finding mathematics irrelevant to their future and being faced with young men who look down at girls who achieve in mathematics.

She has found that mathematics activities involving material that is relevant to her students is more engaging for girls:

> Doing mathematics in my classroom now involves such activities as analyzing water retention of different brands of diapers, which has lead to discussions about why students drop out of school to have babies; constructing different ways to divide 602 M&Ms among 17 hungry students; analyzing a variety of chocolate chip cookies, etc.

Inequities continue in schools in which teachers are not responding to the needs and learning styles of black students (Grant, 1989). Monica, a kindergarten teacher, discusses how the Mathematics Leadership Collaboration helped her to be more responsive to the individual needs of her diverse population of African-American children:

> I began to look more closely and listen more carefully to the mathematical connections that the children made, their individual strategies for solving problems, and the natural math experiences they either brought to the school or they developed in the classroom. I wanted to become more sensitized to the math experiences that happen quite naturally among kindergarten children. I realized, however, that I needed to create an environment where this could occur.

Monica created a classroom that contrasts with those in the working-class schools that Anyon (1980) described. In Monica's classroom children are encouraged to explore and understand the essential elements of mathematics. They share in classroom decisions and management and they contribute to, freely use, and care for classroom materials.

Monica's desire to give children ownership of their classroom, control over their work, and opportunities to make decisions and choices is reflected in details of the physical classroom environment.

- The room is arranged into centers that are changed as the year goes on.
- Children help supply the room with counting materials (e.g., buttons, beans, tops, shells, etc.).
- Shelves are labeled with words and symbols to make locating and returning materials manageable for the children.
- Each child has his/her own wall space where work is displayed.
- Each child has name cards with symbols on cubbies, attendance chart, and the file system.
- Children file all of their own work, return classroom library books to shelves by a color-coded system, and put work in a "share box" to discuss later.

Monica articulates the critical impact of social interaction on learning mathematics. She encourages children to ask the group if and how they agree with one another. In her words, "This sets up a community of learners who respect each other's thinking whether they agree with it or not."

Pamela, too, has found that her students at YALA, formerly dropouts, respond well to cooperative group work and to learning from each other. This may create a link between their ethnicity and social class and "the strategies children learn at home for acquiring, organizing and remembering information" (Grant, 1989, p. 92). Grant used as an example the learning style of African-American students that "tends to be oriented toward cooperation, content about people, discussion and hands-on work, and whole-to-part learning" and notes the conflict between this style and the student-isolating "task-oriented, reading-oriented, part-to-whole style teachers often employ" (p. 92).

As her students work cooperatively, Pamela finds there isn't so much pressure on one student; they don't feel left out or left behind because they can discuss their understandings and problem areas with each other. She finds that they don't feel embarrassed about what they don't know or try to cover it up; instead they tend to stick with a problem until they understand it. They come to see learning as enjoyable and meaningful. She helps them to trust in and value their own thinking as their ideas are listened to and valued by her and other students. She is also actively counteracting the mathematical learning experiences of her students—that if you don't solve a problem quickly, someone else will solve it, give the answer, and your opportunity is over. By concentrating on process rather than correct answers, the students gain time to learn.

This teacher is also concerned with knowledge of space and its connection with mathematical learning. She notes that inner-city children don't have extensive experience with the out-of-doors; they haven't dug holes, gotten lost in the woods, been in expanses of water. They have spent their lives traveling from one inside space to another. She contends that, therefore, they have trouble with such skills as measurement: using a ruler, compass, and straightedge. She finds that experience with these materials is very helpful in their later work with abstract geometric concepts.

As noted in Schram, Wilcox, Lanier, and Lappan (1988), teachers are limited in their ability to teach mathematics by their lack of understanding about how one learns mathematics. When teachers experience learning mathematics by doing it as a member of a cooperative group and have opportunities to discuss their methods and solutions, write about and discuss their own learning process, and then discuss the implications of understandings about the nature of the learning process for their own teaching, teachers begin to look anew at what they are doing with children and often change their teaching practices (Schram et al., 1988; Wilcox, Lanier, Schram, & Lappan, 1992).

In the course of her studies, Pamela reassessed her teaching. This new approach she was using matches what Grant (1989) sees as essential for equitable education: "Involving students actively in classroom activities and in classroom decisions, building on students' learning styles, adapting instruction to the students' skill levels, using cooperative learning, and having teachers who understand and accept the learning styles of the students are baseline essentials for providing educational equity in the classroom" (p. 94).

Pamela reports:

> I try to *engage* students as soon a possible in solving a certain problem, and then develop ideas related to that problem in the course of instruction. I now step back from the problem-solving efforts of my students. . . . Often, when a student figures something out, I require that student to explain it to someone who doesn't understand. This changes the group dynamic, so that students are less dependent on me, and more involved with each other.
>
> I have been using a more investigative approach to math this year. . . . My first assignment was for the students to write a brief essay on a problem they had encountered in life, describing the problem, the tools they used to investigate, and the outcome of their investigation. The essays were then read to the entire class, and we as a class had to decide on the tools of investigation. Some of these tools were very unusual, like courage being used as a tool to investigate another person's character. Our list of tools of investigation included: telephone/telephone book, intuition (figuring out what to do next), bus ticket (a way of getting somewhere), clock/watch (to find out when things happen), newspaper articles (announcing sales, openings at YALA, events of interest), tools for taking equipment apart, salespeople who could give information or aid in securing desired items.

Mathematics Leadership Teams

Students in the Mathematics Leadership Collaboration formed leadership teams in their schools as a prerequisite for joining the program. A central mission of the collaboration was to help teachers to learn to teach mathematics so that more equitable education was achieved. The leadership teams were vehicles for the mathematics leaders to provide materials, curriculum, and ideas about teaching methods that would help their fellow teachers create classroom environments in which *all* children can learn mathematics.

However, the task of running a mathematics leadership team is a complex one. Our students were often taking on formal leadership roles for the first time as they began to meet with their teams. They were in most cases not the most experienced member of their team and they were grappling with new ways of teaching mathematics in their own classrooms. They have come to the team leader role without being an expert in teaching mathematics. They struggle with their role as leader; yet with the support of their advisers, many are creating effective teams and effecting change in their schools. However, in taking this leadership role they have had to clarify and deepen their perceptions of their teaching goals for their own classrooms and the processes that would enable them to achieve these goals.

Monica, a member of the Mathematics Leadership Collaboration, illustrates the possibilities of taking on leadership roles. She begins by discussing the closeness and trust that has developed in her team:

> One of the things that happened recently that I feel really good about is that I gave a workshop for the district on manipulatives. This workshop gave colleagues from the more affluent downtown schools in the district an opportunity to share ideas with teachers from a school from Harlem. I did this in conjunction with two other math team members, a third-grade teacher, and a fourth-grade teacher. We were able to collaborate because we agree about what we can change and what changes need to occur in the classroom. Planning the workshop gave us a shared experience. Forty people attended. The wonderful thing was that people on the math leadership team not involved in presenting the workshop came to support us. They helped to create a climate where people would share with one another.

Particularly around the issues of age and teaching experience, Monica struggles with her role as math leader. It is extremely important that we help teacher leaders understand the role of collaborative leader and model this form of leadership. It is this very notion about classroom teaching that will allow for more equitable education.

Videotapes of mathematics teaching are powerful vehicles for changing classroom practices and fostering collaborative leadership. Teachers who have for the most part learned mathematics through teacher lecture and textbook examples need examples of different approaches so they can free themselves from old images of what it means to learn and teach mathematics. Our mathematics team leaders have made use of commercially made videotapes and those made by teachers in their schools. The latter allow teachers to examine their current teaching practices and to explore the impact of these practices on children's learning. Monica discusses how she has used videotapes in her school.

> One path I've taken with my team and with the school is to show videotapes of exemplary math teaching. The power of the math video is that you are actually seeing math being taught in the classroom setting. You can read about success, but actually seeing it happening in the classroom is very different. It's very powerful because you have that image to walk away with. You see exactly how it is being implemented.

Monica not only has meetings with her team but works individually with teachers, providing them with resources, sometimes working with them in their classrooms, observing their work with children, and inviting them to her classroom. A new first-/second-grade teacher in her school's dual-language program has profited from her support. Grappling with the problems faced by a new teacher was another important step in Monica's growth as a leader.

Another aspect of Monica's leadership work concerned getting her team involved in a joint project. The whole team has been constructing math games, which they are now putting in the library and making available to all classrooms and to parents. They displayed them at a recent parent night in a room that was designed by the fifth graders in the school to allow parents to participate in the kinds of math experiences they are having in their classrooms. In this way, parents experienced something of the contrast to the math by rote they experienced. The teachers on the leadership team are struggling to find ways of helping parents understand new approaches they are using to teach mathematics so they will support the work of their children.

Conclusion

There are several elements common to efforts to make mathematics accessible: The learner brings his or her own thoughts and experiences to the learning situation; children discuss their ongoing work with their peers; concrete materials are used as objects to think with; mathematics is taught through applications that are of interest to the students. We have found this to be true for learners of all ages. In this way, teachers are reaching to accomplish what Grant (1989) promotes in reference to children of color: "Involving students actively in classroom activities and in classroom decisions, building on students' learning styles, adapting instruction to the students' skill levels, using cooperative learning, and having teachers who understand and accept the learning styles of the students are baseline essentials for provident educational equity in the classroom" (p. 94).

Teachers need to value knowledge of children's cultures and prior school experiences, be keen observers of their behaviors and work, know subject matter and a variety of materials and techniques for teaching, and understand the learning process. Teachers engaged in the process of change are challenged by the simultaneous need to apply these concepts in their own classrooms while helping other teachers who have very different ideas about how children learn. Many are steeped in a rote approach to mathematics, understanding mathematics and mathematics teaching to be computation. Although the work with other teachers is difficult for those who are just beginning to incorporate a new approach to the teaching of mathematics, the leadership team approach gives them a discussion group and forum for thinking out loud about their teaching and the new ideas they are struggling with as well as practical knowledge about leadership informed by a concern for equity.

Classroom practices that support mathematics learning include opportunities for discussing mathematics, ongoing assessment of student knowledge, central focus on the child's individual learning and the cultural context he or she brings to school. Our experience in the Mathematics Leadership Collaboration and the reports of Silva and Moses (1990) and of Cole and Griffin (1987) lead us to believe that this approach to mathematics teaching works for females and works for poor minority children as well as it does for the "executive elite" (Anyon, 1980).

References

Anyon, J. (1980). Social class and the hidden curriculum of work. *Journal of Education, 62*(1), 68-91.

Apple, W. A. (1992). Do the standards go far enough? Power, policy, and practice in mathematics education. *Journal for Research in Mathematics Education, 23*(5), 412-431.

Cole, M., & Griffin, P. (Eds.). (1987). *Contextual factors in education.* Madison: University of Wisconsin.

Commission on Standards for School Mathematics. (1989). *Curriculum and evaluation standards for school mathematics* (The Standards). Reston, VA: National Council of Teachers of Mathematics.

Commission on Teaching Standards for School Mathematics. (1991). *Professional standards for teaching mathematics.* Reston, VA: National Council of Teachers of Mathematics.

Fennema, E., & Meyer, M. R. (1989). Gender equity and mathematics. In W. G. Secada (Ed.), *Equity and education* (p. 146-157). New York: Falmer.

Fox, L. H. (1976). Sex differences in mathematical precocity: Bridging the gap. In D. F. Keating (Ed.), *Intellectual talent: Research and development* (pp. 183-214). Baltimore, MD: Johns Hopkins University Press.

Grant, C. A. (1989). Equity, equality, teachers and classroom life. In W. G. Secada (Ed.), *Equity and education* (pp. 89-102). New York: Falmer.

Hsia, J. (1988). *Asian Americans in higher education and at work.* Hillsdale, NJ: Lawrence Erlbaum.

Martin, L. M., & Scribner, S. (1991). Laboratory for cognitive studies of work: A case study of the intellectual implications of a new technology. *Teachers College Record, 92*(4), 582-602.

Meyer, M. R., & Koeler, M. S. (1990). Internal influences on gender differences in mathematics. In E. Fennema and & G. C. Leder (Eds.), *Mathematics and gender* (pp. 60-95). New York: Teachers College Press.

National Research Council. (1989). *Everybody counts.* Washington, DC: National Academy Press.

Rock, D. A., Estrom, R. B., Goertz, M. E., & Plooack, J. (1986). *Study of excellence in high school education: Longitudinal study, 1980-82 final report.* Washington: U.S. Government Printing Office.

Schram, P., Wilcox, S., Lanier, P., & Lappan, G. (1988). *Changing mathematical conceptions of preservice teachers: A content and pedagogical intervention.* East Lansing, MI: National Center for Research on Teacher Education.

Silva, C., & Moses, R. (1990). The algebra project: Making middle school mathematics count. *Journal of Negro Education, 59*(3), 375-391.

Silver, E. (1992). Assessment and mathematics education reform in the United States. *International Journal for Educational Research, 17*(5), 489-502.

Wilcox, S., Lanier, P., Schram, P., & Lappan, G. (1992). *Influencing beginning teachers' practice in mathematics education: Confronting constraints of knowledge, beliefs and context.* East Lansing, MI: National Center for Research on Teacher Education.

8. Breaking Labels and Breaking Promises: The Liberty Partnership at Bank Street College, 1989-1993

DAVID PENBERG

Saw Shawn yesterday. For some unexpected reason he asked me if I was writing a book. I told him, yes, in a manner of speaking, I am. He asked me what it was about. I told him it's on the things I have learned while directing the program. Shawn said, "Just do it well. You should write it so that a teenager can read it and understand what you are saying. This way, it would have value." I will remember what he said to me.

On the first Saturday of our weekend program in fall 1989, Damien Concepcion came to Bank Street College with a Walkman and headphones, baseball cap turned backward. He was armed with a cutting knife and a black marking pen. By the time Jose, the martial arts instructor, disarmed him, Damien had tagged most of the bathrooms from the first to the fourth floor. At the time there was a pathological glint in Damien's eyes. He was one of the few students I have felt had the capacity to do violence at any time. Four years and many cries later, Damien has become one of Jose's prize students. Today, the glowers are gone. He has just completed an intensive course for his SATs (the Princeton Review) and is determined to explore a career in computers. Damien is one of those who could have gone either way. Now instead of rage, there is determination in his eyes. The street bravado is still there, but so is the boy, the inquisitive and caring young man. Still deeply troubled, he is gifted with great pools of energy and focus that he has begun to tap.

We need to ask ourselves what kinds of programs work for adolescents like Damien who is at risk of wasting away underneath their hoods in drug infested parks? What enables him to perservere?

In the life of an adolescent change is often very quiet and incremental. Like the growth of one's own children, change in students seems to occur invisibly in their sleep. It doesn't come in boldface. You need to look carefully for signs of it to notice that Damien never missed one Saturday of the Weekend College. Little by little he shed his Walkman, his headphones, and in time, even removed his baseball cap.

Consider Madelyn, that first summer at Bard College she clutched her teddy bear and was painfully shy. Several years later, she was the spokesperson for our student leadership group, the Advisory Council: She was clear, strong, and speaking with a powerful sense of self. *As educators, what we need to keep in the forefront is that we do not change students. We create the conditions and design the opportunities for them to change themselves.*

Students come to us with so many labels: "at risk," nontraditional, linguistically and culturally diverse, disadvantaged, culturally deprived, poor, inner city, underprivileged, underachieving. Our students spend most of their school lives fulfilling stereotypes and fitting into labels. Such labels do not represent the students we have worked with, for they are not reduced to freeze-dried people. My students have names like cloud formations, diverse and striking: Kimani, Tara, Zuria, Latoya, Nirvanda, Mustafa. They bring with them worlds of resiliency and resourcefulness. Each of the students who has worked with us for the 4 years at Bank Street College is singular and complex. These labels misrepresent them. The story to be told here is about what occurs when you don't label students, what happens when you tear the labels off and allow them to sparkle, expand, and come to life under nourishing and inspiring conditions. The story of the Liberty Partnership Program is about what happens when we enact what we envision.

Decade of the Child

The 1980s were the decade of the child. The capstone program was a state program model fashioned after Eugene Lang's I Have a Dream Foundation. It was called the Liberty Partnerships and offered Liberty Scholarships to a target population of tens of thousands of "at-risk" children in the public schools across New York State. The approach was built around the idea of a consortium: Institutions of higher education, businesses, schools, community-based organizations, and cultural institutions were to come together to develop partnerships designed to enhance the educational opportunities of youth, to guarantee their graduation from high school, and to ensure college for those who completed the program. Each partnership would be customized to meet the needs of a particular community. Each lead institution would remain with its students until the day they graduated.

Fanfare, focus, and money, all there. Ten million dollars allocated in Year 1. Twenty million in Year 2. Thirty million by the third year. Unlike the divisive and finger-pointing *Nation at Risk* that galvanized the nation with more cold war rhetoric, the Liberty Partnerships were ushered in and framed by a governor whose support of and belief in education was unfailing. Fifty-two collaborations were to spring up all across New York from Canton to the Upper West Side of Manhattan, partnerships of colleges and schools, community-based organizations and museums, businesses and parents. The catchword was partnerships; the modus operandi was collaboration.

With the boom years of the early 1980s over, the city and state were left with unpaid bills, leftovers of the Reagan era. The writing was clear on the wall when the Second Annual Liberty Conference in Albany was canceled. The state would renege on the promise it made to thousands of youth and their families. After that the story was consistent. In 1990 the college scholarships were frozen. By the end of the third year, they were eliminated entirely. By 1992 the partnerships had been removed from the governor's budget, later reinstated, but with significant cuts. It was a portrait of how to disassemble a program without even really trying. It was the same old formula of killing the possibility for change before it ever got a chance to take root.

By the end of the second year, with these changes in funding, the partnerships were wounded. They never had a chance to fully work because the changing nature of the partners' fiscal responsibilities was not made clear. Collaborations work when there is a mutual sense of responsibility the partners agree upon. As state fiscal support ebbed and dried up, the financial burdens of the partners were drastically affected. At Bank Street we could never arrive at any equitable distribution for supporting the program. The school district politely refused to pick up any bills. The partners tried, but were themselves financially strapped. After Year 2, the partnership was at risk. Lesson 1: You can't dance if both partners are not moving their feet.

Coordinating the Liberty Partnership at Bank Street: Dreams and Realities

Since fall 1989, as coordinator of Bank Street's Liberty Partnership, I have run this college preparatory program for youth in the corridors and classrooms of Bank Street College. I had just arrived from China after a year teaching English. My family and I had fled the People's Republic when the hopes and banners calling for democracy were crushed after army tanks cleared Tiananmen Square. That same summer the Berlin wall fell and Iraq was in turmoil. It was a season when the whole world seemed to be democratizing. Talk of the peace dividend and a new world order seemed less utopian and more a possibility with each passing day.

As an educator, I have been most interested in elaborating and extending the strategies my own impressive teachers had used, working on ways to inspire young people to ask questions, to use their imaginations, and to take responsibility for their own learning. At the outset of the Liberty Partnership, the prospects of running a joint venture with such a diverse range of educating resources was intriguing. It included: Barnard College, a prestigious, woman's liberal arts college as an after-school tutorial site; the Dome, an established community organization in the Upper West Side, as a site for after-school programming; the New York Historical Society, traditionally elitist and highbrow, as the site for a Saturday enrichment program; and Bard College, an upstate progressive liberal arts college as the site for summer programs. The challenges were alluring for the disparities among the respective institutions as well as for their potential. The Liberty program offered me the opportunity to examine the nature of curriculum and teaching poor, urban youth. It represented a space in which to construct a learning community outside of the boundaries of formal schooling.

My relationship as coordinator was forged between and among disparate actors: students, families, principals and assistant principals, directors, teachers, guidance counselors, security guards, state education officials, foundation officers, and the list goes on. Moving through different groups of people I learned much about talking, communicating, small talk, caring, trusting, clarifying, not trusting, evaluating. I learned a great deal about myself. Liberty was not only about the transformations of young adolescents but also about myself.

"A curriculum [a program] and its pedagogy are versions of our dreams for ourselves, our children, and our communities" (Simon, 1992, p. 122). Liberty was my dream. I dreamed a dream of people and all that I believed mattered in the development of children and adults. What I came increasingly to question was whose dream was I dreaming and how appropriate was it for others. Was it the dream of the students who chose to participate? Was it their parents'? Was it the dream of their teachers and counselors at school? Liberty became the embodiment of my dreams of constructing better, more challenging, more diverse, more ethically grounded lives for children. But whose dream was I dreaming and caretaking? The answer I came up with is that visions, like ideas, take shape in conflict with other moving bodies.

Schools are not ordinary places to visit. Outsiders are often made to feel like outsiders. Going into any of our feeder schools was always a lesson in etiquette, Board of Education style. You just don't come to see a teacher. You must first sign in, see at least two people, and go to the office for a pass. It felt at though I was getting a visa in a foreign consulate. In 4 years I made more phone calls, visited more superintendent's offices, and attended more meetings with 8 1/2 × 11 white pads than I care to remember. Over 4 years there were more struggles, accommodations, responsibilities, compromises, obstacles, growth spurts, miracles, mistakes, judgments, misjudgments, and risks than all my education and prior work experience had ever prepared me for.

Hip Hop Meets Bank Street: First Encounters 1989-1992

We all speak many kinds of language. Some of us are more fluent than others. We are what we wear, how we address each other, interact in an elevator, talk on the phone. We are how we carry ourselves. We are all of these things. This is what defines us as makers and recipients of culture, constructing our identity. When two cultures (foreign; separated by language, racial or ethnic identities, and address) come together there is neither a honeymoon nor an inquisition. Rather there is a process of initiation, of exchange, of conflict, and ultimately of accommodation.

Collaborations are like personal relationships: complex and involving of time and effort if they are going to work. And so it was with Liberty students and the Bank Street community. The encounter was never neat and uncomplicated. The scenarios were memorable: Liberty students with their Walkmans, Air Jordans, and baseball caps; Bank Street with its decorum, its reproving looks, memos of complaint. Most openly embraced and sought involvement with the Liberty students; a few did not and remained distant. Overall, it was an osmosis, a first contact of cultural styles and expectations, perceptions and projections. "Those Liberty kids" were often the first to be blamed when something occurred at the college. By some, they were labeled at Bank Street just as they were at the schools from which they came, as problems to solve or potential troublemakers. When Bank Street opened its doors to the Liberty population, it did not know what it was opening up and what its doors would look like after. The historical mission of the college in serving young children was shaken in its self-assurance when faced by urban black and Latino teenagers. Adolescents brought new and testy challenges to 610 West 112th Street. But cultures that clash can also rub off on each other. How to sensitize different communities of people toward mutuality and regard, how to help bridge gaps, develop trust and ownership, create linkages across the college for greater comprehension and interaction to take place— this was the challenge Liberty brought to Bank Street. It was the challenge I faced as coordinator.

In retrospect there could have been more opportunities for both communities to get to know about each other, to shed stereotypes and fears. Tolerance and understanding don't come about simply by reading something. It requires direct interaction between individuals. We could have set up more arenas for conversation to have taken place. We should have been more forceful in enlisting wider involvement of the Graduate School and the Children's School. With a graduate program in early adolescence and a core of in-service and pre-service teachers to draw on, the Liberty program should have been able to attract a wider arena for these teachers interested in working in public schools on the middle school level. Now I realize that if you place a program of this scope in the middle of an institution, there need to be direct links with other programs across the institution. Liberty should have become an arena for risk taking and curriculum exploration. It should have been a fulcrum for the college's work with public schools, a kind of model that said, "See this is what is possible; this is what can be done." These things did not happen.

On the other hand, there were small victories, incremental changes. Partnerships are processes "whose outcomes are never really clear" (Sirotnic & Goodlad, 1988, pp. 12-13). They are social experiments in which, through inquiry and problem solving, we find better ways of doing things. The process of osmosis worked both ways. Working and living together (using the same classrooms, spaces, elevators, libraries) requires not only communication and understanding, but also shifts in behavior. It is difficult to avoid stereotypes and build on a mutual respect and acknowledgment of differences, but commitment to a partnership, with constant interaction and joint tasks, can lead to reconceptualizations and to the mutual benefit of both. Four years is a short span in the world of people and institutions. In that time Bank Street College learned as much from the relationships as the Liberty students derived from the institution, working in the Family Center as interns, interacting with graduate students and the children's school and as counselors in the children's after-school program. The desirable nature of collaborations like Liberty, despite their complexity and unanticipated complications, lies in the way they can bring cultures together and make a community more aware of itself and more diversified.

Reap What You Sow

The state calls it attrition: the "inactives." The files of students who stop coming to programs like Liberty go the way of boxes, stored in basements with labels on them. They get removed from the "actives list" and for all purposes (except as numbers) they cease to exist. But to those who work with youth, the students have names and lives that if we allow it, leave their imprint on us. They are those who got away, slipped through the cracks, fell through the net; those that no follow-through or follow-up can ever retrieve. They come and go, appear and disappear, like shooting stars. Augusto, Solomon, Yvette. The litany is like the roll call of soldiers missing in action. I often wonder if Juan is still painting, creating those exacting, wondrous portraits. Is Augusto still shooting video? And Solomon, is he still practicing martial arts? And David, our Paul Robeson of the streets, who had a problem with stealing. The image of him, shirtless, body taut and sculpted like Apollo's doing Shakespeare with the confidence of a rap song.

Where do they disappear to? What do they take and retrieve from programs like these? Why do they leave us with disconnected phones, no return address, and without ever saying good-bye? Students' lives get inside of your own life. Young people endear themselves to you. Where do they go? Where are they now? How do we let them fall into cracks and out of our lives? What calls them away—concern for their family, the pull of the street, discouragement from life's complexities?

Contexts

The majority of Liberty students attend schools that are terribly ordinary places. Their learning takes place in overheated buildings that resemble the housing projects where they live—impersonal, concrete, linear places. It sometimes feels as if the public agencies, in this case, the Board of Education and the Housing Authority, conspire to make school buildings and public housing as dreary and uninspiring places as possible. On occasion, these ordinary places have extraordinary teachers among the ordinary ones, not bad or evil people, but ones whose work has lost distinction.

Many Liberty students have guidance counselors who don't return phone calls and who always seem to be in meetings. Too frequently, they are people who appear uncomfortable in the company of these children, and relying on labels, erect walls between us and them. These are teachers who in counseling children deprive them of their giftedness and their voices. Liberty students go to schools where there are too many people like these guidance counselors—who instead of advocating and encouraging students, fail them.

The need for programs like Liberty lies not only in what schools do to children, but also in what they don't do for them. Instead of encouragement, opportunities, and choices, they come with "impairments, weaknesses, and deficits." It is no wonder that schools and parks suffer from the same visible evidence of young people's rage and anger, the consequences of what it is like to be perceived as something inferior, someone at risk.

The job of adolescents seems to be to test and stretch the limits of what is acceptable, just as it is the task of those adults who either live or work with them to set limits, to create boundaries. It took close to 2 years of coming late, loud Walkmans, beepers, scattered graffiti, and isolated instances of theft for trust to be welded. Programs do not forge trust, just as scholarly articles do not create learning communities. Teachers like Maureen, Edna, Luis, Jose, Pam were there every Saturday. These were people who became our foundation. What Liberty was able to provide in the lives of these students, whose lives were often unstable and uncertain, was a sense of continuity, a continuity of place and people.

Maxine Greene talks of creating public spaces "where diverse beings come together to articulate their concerns and to even take action to make change" (Greene, 1992, p. 17). This is the kind of space we tried to create at Bank Street. People like Pam, Maureen, Joe cultivated relationships with students in classes where students learned to speak to one another in a way that was imbued with care, trust, and endless discussions. Learning communities are places where people care. They are delicate ecosystems of adults, children, and families mutually supporting, challenging, and affirming each other. Learning communities comprise first and foremost people: adults who by experience and predilection speak to and inspire young people. There is no great mystery to this. Expose youth to adults who are excited and engaged by what they do and chances are this will be transmitted to youth. Expose students to teachers who would rather be reading the newspaper, hiding behind the threat of tests, grades, and textbooks and chances are the students will be bored, antagonistic, and committed to resistance. We built our program around people passionate about their own work as writers, teachers, filmmakers, and dancers.

You create a sense of belonging when you are made to feel welcomed. Bank Street became, over time, that kind of place. Learning communities are not textbooks. They don't come ready made or in neat sequential packages. By their nature they evolve, change, take root. Commonality of goals and mutuality of needs come about when youth are provided spaces to communicate ideas and have responsibilities to take on.

Cornel West talks of the "nihilism" that defines the lives of black communities "the lived experience of coping with a life of meaninglessness, hopelessness and (most importantly) love-less" (*The New York Times*, 1993, p. 26). He is referring to the world that many of the Liberty Scholars inhabit, where best friends are killed, drive-by shootings are common, and to con-template dealing and running of drugs is a common choice.

Liberty was designed, from the curriculum to the staffing, as an alternative space to public school, as a structure where meaning and feeling could be sustained through the values of diligence, service, care, discipline, and excellence. As a learning community we were not built on the remediation of young people, but in channeling their transformations. The ethos was one of enrichment, not deficiency. Students came to the Liberty program not because they had to but because they chose to. What students derived from the program was as diverse as their needs and personalities. For Kimani it was a way of growing into a leader. The program gave him the opportunities to take on responsibilities as a spokesperson and a peer counselor as well as the skills attendant to working with and leading others. For others like Mustafa, Renee, and Madelyn, Liberty offered the support they needed and the space to grow into leadership roles. The Advisory Council, the residential summer program at Bard, and for those few who could participate, travel to China and Central America, all were challenges to hone skills and polish abilities to communicate, solve problems, and collaborate.

For the Lisas, Zurias, and Latoyas the program represented a way to gather their inner resources and inner strengths through counseling to overcome difficult and divisive family situations. The program encouraged them to take risks, speak out, and to take on responsibilities. They came to learn how to deal with family traumas without being overwhelmed and absorbed by them. They learned to convert their energy into their own educational and social development, and by confronting adversity and collective problem solving, they developed strategies for overcoming them.

For young African-American males like Germaine, Vincent, and Akil it was a place to come and play ball. It was a program where you could get something to eat, with no posses in the halls. A place to get tutoring, if you wanted. "A place to chill" where they would feel at home, less vulnerable, more at ease. It was a place where they were not removed from class, not labeled, a place where they could seek assistance if they so chose and where the idea of college became a reachable and feasible reality if they chose to accept the challenge.

For Damien, it was Sam. Someone to reach out to, break through the macho defense. Sam was an adult who could grab him, tell him "Son, its okay to be angry." He would say to a student in rage, "Let it out" or, "I'm here to listen." For young people like Damien, Liberty was a pathway out of anger, despair, and eternal punkhood. For Damien, the summer program at Bard College was seminal. It was his first immersion in a rigorous academic environment in which it was okay to participate. For Damien the program also was a chance, through Jose and martial arts, to channel his anger, his insecurities through the art of self-defense. It was a way of achieving self-respect through self-discipline.

The students came on Saturdays, during the week, and during the summer. They came because we cajoled them. They came because their friends came. They came because they made a deliberate choice to come. They came because it was better than Saturday cartoons or doing laundry for their mother. They came because it was different. It was not school, but it was school. "They made learning fun. They explained what we didn't understand at school."

They came to review their math or English or science skills. They came to watch movies and to talk about them. They came to talk about the things that matter in their lives: boyfriends and girlfriends, sexuality, drugs, jobs, college, life in the neighborhood, life in school, parents, friends. They came to listen and speak to each other and to speak with adults who would not judge them, who always had the time to be there. They came to make photographs, visit exhibitions, attend conferences. They came to write books; write articles; investigate family histories; construct family trees; create maps, sculptures, wall murals. They came to write on word processors, review sequential math and global history. They came on their own volition. Their own choice. They came here because of their commitment to set goals for themselves. They came because of their desire to develop themselves into critical, caring, literate, and responsible human beings.

They came because they were respected and in being respected were challenged. They came because we chose to see them as full of giftedness and not as risks. They came because of their willingness to take responsibility for their own lives, their own learning. They came because they were welcomed. They came because they said no to Saturday morning cartoons, vandalism, drug dealing, unwanted pregnancy, jumping subway turnstiles, racism. They came to get counseling and to write plays, college essays, a newsletter. They came to do martial arts, review sequential math 2, tutor peers, make documentaries, attend advisory councils. They kept coming because of the Sams and Stuarts and Maureens and Afias who listened when they spoke, who brought diligence and enthusiasm to their work, and who demanded the same of them. They came for 4 years and still keep coming to a program that took them seriously and held high expectations for them. They came to a place that gave them security, promised them hope, and offered them windows to the future.

There is a series of photographs of Liberty students and staff in a wide expansive circle visiting the Eleanor Roosevelt Estate in Valhalla, New York. It is early fall 1990, and all of the Summer

Academy participants (Bard) have reunited. Students and staff are holding hands while it drizzles in a landscape full of Thanksgiving colors. Somehow the image of this circle between adults and youth is representative of what we came to create: a learning community; a complex ecosystem of youth, teachers, and parents working together toward a common set of goals, engaging young people in the process of questioning their future identities and possibilities.

In Retrospect

Mustafa tells me: "Liberty has been like an aspirin to me. I've been coming here because there are adults who will listen, who have time for you. You want to know if programs like these work—just compare me with one of my friends not in the program. That will tell you. People care about you here. That makes a difference."

Programs like these cannot be packaged because they must fit the people for whom the program has been created. There are no quick fixes. Four years ago at the outset of the program we were poised to create something special. Some of the guiding principles and questions that informed our pedagogy and approach were:

1. *Take adolescents seriously and they will excel.* Adolescents have a need and desire to be in the world (spray paint on it if need be) and not be handed a textbook rendering of it.

2. *Take care in creating the environment.* Create a program that uses a college, a place where learning and teaching are esteemed and valued, to create opportunities and structures for young people to express, explore, and develop themselves as literate and responsible human citizens.

3. *Make maximum use of people resources.* Expose young people to adults who are inspired and active about their own work.

4. *Build on giftedness, not deficits.* Construct a program that challenges and draws on multiple ways of knowing the world for young adolescents, where they can acquire in-

formation and knowledge through varieties of mediums, disciplines, and people.

For the last 4 years I've had the distinct privilege of witnessing the alchemizing of young lives, the burgeoning of self-confidence, and the budding of talent. Eschewing prescriptions and deficit models, we drew on and brought out the curiosity and initiative of adolescents. My story is also Kimani's, Tara's, Tyronne's, Damien's, Mustafa's, and the stories of the families and of the staff. It is my story, too. It is a chronicle of individual victories and private dramas. The story of programs like these is superimposed with individual odysseys through subways, unsafe neighborhoods, abusive homes, leaden schools, and welfare offices seeking freedom from the onus of labels and limited chances of becoming successful adults. When all the statistics, reports, and tables are laid to some eternal bureaucratic rest in some dusty basement, what remains are memorable names and stories.

Kimani, speaking loudly and with pride to an assembly full of peers about his grandmother's life as a sharecropper; Mustafa eloquently explaining in Albany to state legislators and their aides why programs like Liberty work and what would occur without them; Madelyn as spokesperson for our student leadership group in the Advisory Council: clear, strong, and speaking with a powerful sense of self; Tyronne, in suit and tie inside the juvenile justice court awaiting his fate in the hands of an irate, impatient judge; Latoya returning from the disappeared after a year on the streets. My story is the chronicle of how the Tyronnes, Latoyas, and Jesuses move from the cycles of failure and misdirected and underachieving lives into citizens who grow up with the belief that they too can have significant lives—provided we can create and sustain the places for these miracles to happen and persuade others to support them.

Postscript

On April 6, 1993, the Liberty Partnership program was again restored for the second time in 2 years to the state budget. Its

allocation was even increased, granting it another year of life
until the next round of budget crises. The promise of a college
education was an integral part of the program at its inaugura-
tion. What the students heard was, "You participate in this
program, graduate from high school, and we will pay for your
college education (at least a portion of it)." The year 1993 was
to have been the capstone year with a budget of $40 million.
Instead, the budget is now $7.3 million and there continues to
be the question of total elimination.

Like the other Liberty Partnership program directors, I have
had to ask what it means to the students and their families to
watch the erosion of support and the potential of their dreams
disappear. It has been difficult to live with the uncertainty of
year-by-year funding and doubly difficult to maintain momen-
tum with the students during the periods of campaigning for
continuance. For like the others, I knew that to abandon these
students midway would be serious indeed.

The program goals for the Liberty Partnerships are not unique.
Across the country are many carefully designed dropout pre-
vention programs. Most depend on public funding, typically
through school district allocation. As legislatures, administrations, educators contemplate the needs and stresses caused by
poverty, unemployment, illness and attempt to make individual marks on programs, the flow of money is affected. Like the
participants in Liberty, others experience truncated programs
and concomitant reaction to broken promises.

This is not another chronicle of gloom. We already have
enough to constitute a war memorial to the burned out and
alienated of our public schools. Four years later the first class
of approximately 75 seniors are about to graduate.

Don't we need more programs like these? I believe the insights of 16-year-old Mustafa eloquently answer this:

> These kinds of programs are essential. . . . It's almost as if they
> were food. If you don't have food you can't function, and if you
> don't have a Liberty Program where there's somebody that cares
> about you, where you can go and say my teacher isn't teaching me

what I'm suppose to learn, or I don't think I'm gonna do well in this school, or I need tutoring in math. You know. *Who are you to go to?*

I really don't comprehend why they cut these programs. Because we live in a . . . society where everything is about money. Education . . . it's like down there with sneakers. People need to know that programs like this are essential. . . . If you take this from me, you might as well take my breath. . . . It's sort of like a mental livelihood that I have. If you take that from me, you might as well take everything that I know. *Leave me ignorant . . . because it will just make me frustrated.*

Partnerships, like learning, flourish when they can be *substained over time*. We need to contemplate the effects of our broken promises.

References

Greene, M. (1992). Perspective and diversity: Toward a common ground. In F. Pignatelli & S. W. Pflaum (Eds.), *Celebrating diverse voices* (pp. 1-20). Newbury Park, CA: Corwin.

Simon, R. (1992). *Teaching against the grain: Texts for a pedagogy of possibility.* New York: Bergin & Garvey.

Sirotnik, K. A., & Goodlad, J. I. (Eds.). (1988). *School-university partnerships in action: Concepts, cases, and concerns.* New York: Teachers College Press.

The New York Times. (1993, April 2). P. 26.

9. Talking About Equity and Excellence

HERBERT KOHL

Recently a number of scholars including Barbara Christian (1985), Henry Lewis Gates, Jr. (1986), and William Ayers (1989), have chosen to approach complex social and legal issues through the medium of telling and analyzing fables, dialogues, and stories. They also use anecdotes and interviews to approach abstract argument through concrete instances. This choice is a conscious comment on what they believe are the limitations imposed by argument from theory. Their goal is to explore the complexity of issues such as racism and the determination of what is equitable that cannot be settled solely by rational argument. They try to include feelings and passions in their analyses and to mine the widest range of opinion to discover the nuances of folly and wisdom that contribute to the making of theory. They also create a place in their analysis for the expression of their own opinions and for speculation on their experience. In doing this they deliberately blur the distinction between professional and lay speculation. It is a way of coming out of the academy and joining public debate rather than being content to address their work solely to the academic community.

These people's work provides models educators should attend to as issues as central to education as equity and excellence are as value laden as any faced in the law or psychology. Equity is a question of values and excellence a matter of judgment. At the heart of commitment to equity is the sentiment that what is just and what is legal do not necessarily coincide, and that struggling for justice demands resisting or changing laws if they conflict with one's notion of justice. This implies appeal to moral rather than political or legal authority. However, appeal to moral authority does not involve statute, citation, or precedent. Rather it is a matter of vision, commitment to ideas of good and evil, and decisions to act on the side of good.

In the case of determining what is excellent there are similarly personal and cultural commitments to a notion of what is best that goes beyond objective formulation and certitude. Therefore arguing for a particular stance on equity or specific definition of excellence is as much a matter of rhetoric, story telling, and anecdote as it is a question of marshaling evidence and producing chains of reasoning. For these reasons it is very important that educators look to other fields where the domain of objectivity has been challenged and new spaces for advocacy and argument have been created.

In civil law Derrick Bell is one of the most prominent of these scholars, as Robert Coles (1986) is in cultural and psychological studies of youth. Bell's (1989, 1992) books deal with issues such as affirmative action, equity, school busing, integration, and the persistence of racism. Bell (1989) describes why he chose to break with the usual way of producing legal argument:

> The heroine of my book, Geneva Crenshaw, and her Chronicles owe their being to America's most prestigious legal periodical, the *Harvard Law Review*, and its annual practice of inviting a legal scholar to write the foreword to the Supreme Court issue. . . . I wanted to examine from a new perspective—beyond even the most exacting exegesis of case decisions—the civil rights movement since 1954 and the *Brown* school decision: that is, to explain or justify what has happened, or not happened, and how black people (or some of us) feel about it.
>   The civil rights movement is, after all, much more than the totality of the judicial decisions, the antidiscrimination laws, and the changes in racial relationships reflected in those legal

milestones.The movement is a spiritual manifestation of the continuing faith of a people who have never truly gained their rights in
a nation committed by its basic law to the freedom of all. For my
foreword, then, I sought a method of expression adequate to the
phenomenon of rights gained, then lost, then gained again. . . .
There came to my rescue Geneva Crenshaw and her tales, challenging the accepted view of how blacks gain, or might gain
from civil rights laws and policies. (pp. xi-xii)

Robert Coles's approach is equally unorthodox in many ways,
though Coles's work does not cause the kind of controversy that
Bell provokes. In a series of books Coles relates stories about
the feelings, observations, and opinions of children he has
observed and taped. Most often he includes himself in the tales
and lets the reader in on his opinions and feelings. Coles is a
compassionate man, not an activist like Bell, but a person of
enormous sympathy across class, race, and culture. However,
there are times when he uses his stories to attack universalizing
theories about child development and growth. For example, he
will tell the tales of specific children and the way they functioned under crisis as a vehicle for attacking dogmatic commitments to Piagetian developmental stage theories. Or he
might illustrate how Freudian thought is inadequate to explain early childhood motivations by presenting specific tales
of children choosing to risk their lives in civil rights struggles.
Coles does not provide much countertheorizing, but sets parameters for a fuller and more respectful view of child development that does not claim or need to explain everything. Coles
(1986) provides an example of how he works to transform the
way people talk about the psychology and cultural analysis of
childhood:

I have before me, as I write these words, a weathered old piece of
hospital paper, and on it a remark typed by a woman who spent
her days listening to my ilk talk and talk and talk—so that she
might "transcribe" what we said. "The patient says a lot of people
like Ike.". . .
    My wife, going over all this with me later, had her own opin-
ion of what the typist . . . had "really" meant to say: that some of

us, in the name of our own political values, meant to be the spokes-persons of others—the poorer folk who (we were sure) would be better served by a victory of Stevenson and the Democratic Party; but the typist, whose *lot* some of us, in the abstract, worried over long and hard, . . . wanted me to stop and think. Do "you," after all, know what he means—what anyone means—when saying "I like Ike"? . . .

I go into this long windup, with all its political, professional, sociological implications, because for me *The Political Life of Children* began right then—when an anxious child began to teach a young doctor that there most assuredly was a political life among children. (pp. 7-9)

I have quoted Bell and Coles because their informal and anec-dotal route to analysis makes sense in approaching the question of how multiculturalism can be seen as an issue of equity and excellence. Bell views law as a contest, but one of the many arenas where issues of equity are played out. Coles see children as sensitive actors who are creative in their responses to experience. They both focus on that space where decision is possible, moral choice is necessary, and change can take place. To respect the complexity of that space they choose to begin with the particu-lar—the story, interview, dialogue, anecdote, fable. They deal with questions that have no set answers but are contested as people in our society struggle to decide how they will treat each other. Equity is one such question. Secada characterizes equity in the following way:

The heart of equity lies in our ability to acknowledge that, even though our actions might be in accord with a set of rules, their *results* may be unjust. Equity goes beyond following the rules, even if we have agreed that they are intended to achieve jus-tice. . . . Educational equity, therefore, should be construed as a check on the justice of specific actions that are carried out within the educational arena and the arrangements that result from those actions. (quoted in Pignatelli & Pflaum, 1992, p. ix)

"Equity goes beyond following the rules." It is precisely that character that makes a study of equity beg for anecdotal treat-ment as well as analysis. To struggle for equity sometime means to struggle against the law or the common assumptions of the community. It makes people who try to fight equity issues particularly sensitive to the personal and sometimes religious and moral values that drive their actions. And it makes them adapt to being in opposition. It is not simply a matter of reason or theory. Equity is a passionate issue and it engages the passions of people who struggle for it. As Martin Luther King, Jr., said in a speech he gave at the University of California in Berkeley,

> Modern psychology has a word that is probably used more than any other word. It is the word "maladjusted." Now we all should seek to live a well-adjusted life in order to avoid neurotic and schizophrenic personalities. But there are some things within our social order to which I am proud to be maladjusted and to which I call upon you to be maladjusted. I never intend to adjust myself to segregation and discrimination. I never intend to adjust myself to mob rule. I never intend to adjust myself to the tragic effects of the methods of physical violence and to tragic militarism. I call upon you to be maladjusted to such things. (quoted in Washinton, 1992, p. 33)

The notion of excellence is equally contentious. A glimpse at the history of standardized group testing is instructive in this context. The first was constructed in 1910 by the psychologist Edward Thorndike. It was a test of handwriting. Thorndike collected over 20,000 samples of handwriting by fifth through eighth graders. He also selected about 50 people whom he considered expert judges of handwriting and gave them samples to rank in order of excellence, from 1 to 10. He assumed that it was possible to make this ranking and set up standards of excellence that make one wonder about the whole business of ranking.

Once a test such as this one is created, however, some educators draw conclusions that affect children's lives. For example, because handwriting can presumably be measured, schools might be required to teach to Level 10 rather than help each student develop a legible, fluid, and personal style of writing. Handwriting textbooks might be (and were) created to conform to Thorndike's standards.

I remember the torture of handwriting classes in elementary school, of writing with a standard pen and nib and having to be careful not to get ink all over my hands and shirt. I also remember being judged according to the "standard" of excellent writing set by my teachers. I didn't come up to it and was a constant B–, though I believe my Level 7 handwriting is quite legible and reflects my character better than the narrow, slanted, more formal script of Level 10.

In addition to Thorndike's work on handwriting, standards for English composition and arithmetic were also being worked on during the 1910s. Embodied in these early efforts was the idea that intelligence and academic achievement could somehow be related, and that every subject must have a unique hierarchical structure ranging in steps from better to best. The idea that there might be many forms of excellence, which is at the center of attempts to develop exhibitions and portfolios, was not entertained by the original test makers.

Great impetus was given to the test-making and test-giving industry during World War I when the U.S. Army adopted a series of group tests to decide who was fit for service, who should be channeled to menial and grunt labor, and who should be sent to officers' training school. From September 1917 to January 1919, the army tested 1,726,960 people, including all men called up in the white draft and colored draft (there were two separate drafts into the segregated army) as well as 42,000 commissioned officers. Individual examinations were given to 82,000 men. Thus began the enormous growth of the educational psychology business and the testing industry.

The results of the army tests are fascinating. College-educated, upper-middle- and upper-class individuals performed best and were chosen as officers because of their presumed superiority in intelligence. Working-class and poor men were put in the infantry and sent to the front lines. Blacks were channeled to menial roles serving the white military establishment. Of course, the test makers and test givers were educated, white, middle-class men who wrote the test from the perspective of their worlds, and from their position of power did not consider this a biasing factor. One underlying assumption, for example, was that excellence in reading, writing, and other school-related skills was a good predictor of military leadership, though if I had to serve I'd rather be under someone who had 15 years' experience leading a construction gang than someone who had put in 15 years on Chaucer.

In a distressing quote from his book on the development of standardized testing Pintner (1924) said in reference to the African Americans who took his tests, "all results show the Negro decidedly inferior to the white on standard intelligence tests." (p. 243)

It is interesting that recently it has been shown that many of the results Pintner based his conclusions on were falsified, and the tests themselves shown to be inadequate and biased.

It may be that these class- and race-bound results of tests were not built into the tests and surprised the test makers. However, there is some evidence that bias was intentionally built into early tests. W.E.B. DuBois, in a 1925 issue of *Crisis*, mentions that a battery of achievement tests were given to blacks and whites in Louisville. The blacks did as well as the whites and therefore the results were embarrassing to the whites. The tests were withdrawn and "renormed," a euphemism for saying readjusted so the results would come out right.

Another specific instance of setting norms of excellence as a social and political act was described recently (Synnott, 1979). It seems that in 1919, Columbia University was worried about having too many Jewish students. They therefore adopted the Tests for Mental Alertness devised by E. L. Thorndike of Teachers College, the same man who developed the handwriting test, partly on the assumption that "objectionable" applicants would not have "had the home experiences which enable them to pass these tests as successfully as the average American boy" (p. 248). They succeeded at least temporarily in lowering Jewish admissions.

A common factor in struggles for equity and against an exclusive interpretation of excellence is the need to separate sensibility and judgment from pseudo-claims to objectivity and dogmatic appeals to established authority.

Equity at the School

Struggles for equity against the law or the pressure of common opinion are definitely forms of maladjustment and causes of conflict and pain. They take place in the singular and the particular, though afterward it is possible to speculate on their structure and implications. And when they focus on issues of multiculturalism they raise community as well as individual passions in which both sides mobilize the rhetoric of equality and invoke the spirit of democracy. I have been involved in many struggles over equity. Sometimes they develop in the most unexpected and strange ways.

A number of years ago I visited an elementary school in southern Texas. In the hallway opposite the principal's office there was an elaborate, commercially manufactured display welcoming students, parents, and visitors to the school. The slogan of the display, "Great things happen to children like ours," was spelled out in letters 3 feet high. Under the letters were four larger-than-life cutout figures of children. They were all white, three had blue eyes, two had blonde hair, and the other two sandy brown hair. The children were beaming with pride and they all had handsome briefcases and shiny lunch boxes. The principal pointed out the exhibit to me and beamed proudly at what he described as an expression of school spirit.

The school was in an economically depressed neighborhood and 100% of the students were Mexican, Mexican American, or Chicano. There was not one child who looked anything like any of the children on the walls. Most of the students in the school were on the free lunch program and didn't bring lunch boxes to school. A few of the children did have briefcases, however.

I pointed these things out to the principal and said that this might present a negative image to the students and the community. He told me that I didn't understand. The children on the wall were models for his student body, examples of what they could achieve if only they tried. I was a guest and so I didn't ask him whether his idea was that the school should provide hair dye, briefcases, and a middle-class income for all of his students' families. However, I asked him what he imagined the students thought about seeing those models day after day and knowing that they didn't look like any children at the school. At that point he launched into a tirade against multicultural-ism, told me his goal was to make the school monolingual in English, and chattered away about the good old days when students tried to do their work and parents supported the administration. These days, he concluded, students can't learn and parents just don't care. He assured me that his staff had done everything in their power to make the students learn, but the students just weren't up to the demands of education in the United States. At that point I asked him if all of the students were recent immigrants as he had implied and he stared at me blankly. I was invited to the school by a number of parents and two teachers whose families had lived in that community for generations.

I didn't pursue the issues with him, but did spend time with the parents and teachers who had invited me to visit the school. During our conversations the parents expressed extreme frus-tration. The teachers characterized the overall feeling about the children's school careers as one of depression. I wasn't sure what they meant by depression and asked them to explain in specific ways the dynamics of their distress. Their explanations, which emerged during several days of conversation, had di-rectly to do with the conflicts between their view of equity and the principal's view of equality.

For the principal equality meant that every child had the same opportunity to read the same textbooks, take the same tests, and answer the same questions in class. The content of the texts, the nature of the test questions, and the skew of teacher expectations were not factors that the principal felt might inter-fere with or actually inhibit learning. Nor was an under-standing of the cultural strengths of the parent community relevant to the question of how students might succeed in school.

For the parents and the two teachers these issues were cen-tral. For them considerations of equity were more important than those of equality. They believed that the equal opportunity to read biased texts was not equitable. In fact, they knew it insulted and punished their children. They felt that the school was making their smart children ignorant. The word "their" was operative. The children were not just students thrown into a system of competition that would judge their competence and channel their futures. The children were the future, the hope to create better lives and at the same time maintain personal and cultural integrity. Very few of the parents had any intention of giving up allegiance to their Mexican origins or the Spanish language. They had relatives across the border and lived in two countries, spoke two languages, and lived within one cultural tradition while entering another. Multiculturalism was a matter of everyday existence for them and their children. The equity issue was how the reality of their existence would be honored by the school their children attended. It was a question of how respect for the children could pervade the way in which they were taught and the subjects they were taught.

Their depression was caused to a considerable degree because they knew better than the school people and the textbooks the history of Mexico and Texas—they had relatives who made it or were victims of it. Textbook misrepresentations were not mere factual errors or omissions, but direct and unambiguous insults. When for example, the junior high school textbook they showed me claimed that "the first people to settle Texas came from New England and Virginia," the community and the children were insulted. When children who had come from decent schools in Mexico were given math word problems in English and judged deficient in math because they couldn't solve them, the situation was depressing.

Children of Mexican origin in this community were put in a position, in math and throughout the curriculum, where they couldn't prove what they knew and were treated as intellectually deficient because of the cultural biases of the system. The depression was a covert acknowledgment of the lack of equity in their children's education. Equity would mean their children would be honored for the people they are and welcomed to participate in a complex democracy that had high regard for them. The reality is that their children are being asked to give up pride and self-respect as the price of being processed into pretend democracy.

This is not just the condition of people of Mexican origin in Texas. African-American people live in a multicultural world whether or not their children go to schools where multiculturalism is central to the curriculum. Any attempt to retreat from multiculturalism in the schools has to confront the over 400 year history of the development of African-American culture. This development has taken place within hostile white cultures that are the subject of many African-American cultural strategies for survival. The question is not whether people's lives are multicultural, but whether the society and the schools honor that fact and don't confuse democratic citizenship with cultural conformity. Making that confusion is done at the cost of rejecting equity in life and in school.

Sources From Stories

The understanding of equity issues is embodied in people's tales and jokes. Many of these tales are continually updated and provide a running commentary on the state of equity at a given time. For example, there is a powerful and imaginative story created within the community of enslaved African Americans during the time of slavery. It is about people who could fly and is a remarkable tale of the free spirit and mind that despite enslavement dreams of a world in which equity is an overriding principle. It is also a tale of escape and liberation, as accessible to 5-year-olds as to adults. The story told slaves that they came from a great people and must remember who they are and continue to dream of what they can be. It was an affirmation of culture in the midst of attempts to eradicate it. It kept people's minds "fixed on freedom" and taught multiculturalism to the children of slaves—that is, it taught of the culture of the master and of the abiding cultural values and dreams of their African ancestry.

Here is a very condensed version of Virginia Hamilton's (1989) telling of the tale in her book *The People Could Fly:*

They say the people could fly. Say that long ago in Africa, some of the people knew magic. And they would walk up on the air like climbing up on a gate. And they flew like blackbirds over the fields. Black, shiny wings flappin against the blue up there.

Then, many of the people were captured for Slavery. The ones that could fly shed their wings. They couldn't take their wings across the water on the slave ships. Too crowded, don't you know.

The folks were full of misery, then. Got sick with the up and down of the sea. So they forgot about flyin when they could no longer breathe the sweet scent of Africa.

Say the people who could fly kept their power, although they shed their wings. They kept their secret magic in the land of slavery. . . .

One such who could was an old man, call him Toby. And standin tall, yet afraid, was a young woman who once had wings. Call her Sarah. Now Sarah carried a babe tied to her back. She trembled to be so hard worked and scorned. . . .

Sarah hoed and chopped the row as the babe on her back slept. Say the child grew hungry. That babe started up bawling too loud. Sarah couldn't stop to feed it. Couldn't stop to soothe and quiet it down. She let it cry. She didn't want to. She had no heart to croon to it.

"Keep that thing quiet," called the Overseer. He pointed his finger at the babe. The woman scrunched low. The Driver cracked his whip across the babe anyhow. The babe hollered like any hurt child, and the woman fell to the earth.

The old man that was there, Toby, came and helped her to her feet.

"I must go soon," she told him.

"Soon," he said.

Sarah couldn't stand up straight any longer. She was too weak. The sun burned her face. The babe cried and cried, "Pity me, oh, pity me," say it sounded like. Sarah was so sad and starvin, she sat down in the row.

"Get up, you black cow," called the Overseer. He pointed his hand, and the Driver's whip snarled around Sarah's legs. Her sack dress tore into rags. Her legs bled onto the earth. She couldn't get up.

Toby was there where there was no one to help her and the babe.

"Now, before it's too late," panted Sarah. "Now, Father!"

"Yes, Daughter, the time is come," Toby answered. "Go, as you know how to go!"

He raised his arms, holding them out to her. "*Kum . . . yali, kum buba tambe*," and more magic words, said so quickly, they sounded like whispers and sighs.

The young woman lifted one foot on the air. Then the other. She flew clumsily at first, with the child now held tightly in her arms. Then she felt the magic, the African mystery. Say she rose just as free as a bird. As light as a feather. (p. 170)

The People Could Fly celebrates the spirits who had the strength to flee slavery and teaches about the inner preparation that precedes the physical act of risking one's life for freedom. Though its message can be understood by everyone it has a special cultural and personal significance for African Americans. Although there is no more institutionalized slavery in the United States, much of the substance of slavery (such as economic dependency) is perpetuated through racism and the violence of poverty that still characterizes life in the United States for many African-American people. The need to fly away from racist oppression to develop a full and free life persists, and therefore the need for stories about freedom and the strength of the imagination to overcome depression and despair is as strong as ever. Not surprisingly, therefore, stories of flying people have been revived and retold.

The artist and storyteller Faith Ringgold has transformed the tale into a moving and inspiring story for young children in her (1991) book *Tar Beach*. The central character in the story tells us toward the beginning of the book, "I can fly—yes, fly. Me, Cassie Louis Lightfoot, only eight-years-old and in the third grade, and I can fly. That means I am free to go wherever I want for the rest of my life."

In the course of the book, Cassie tells us how she is going to make her father rich and stop her mother from crying all winter over the frustrations and humiliations her husband goes through because he can't get into the union and have a decent job. Cassie also tells us how she'll make sure the family gets ice cream desserts for dinner and even agrees to teach her brother how to fly. At the end of the book she addresses the reader and says: "Anyone can fly. All you need is somewhere to go that you can't get to any other way. The next thing you know, you're flying among the stars." I have read this book with 5- and 6-year-olds and they all loved Cassie. They understood the metaphor of flying as an image of their own potential freedom whether they were African American or not. And they understood that the world was not fair to Cassie's dad or mom, that equity was a matter of struggle and not a given.

The Impact of Cultural Hegemony

When confronting the demands of society, simple equality is not enough if implicit in the notion of equality is the repudiation of one's birthright. If equality means that everyone has an equal chance to admire the monocultural dreams of Western Europeans and be tested on the misrepresentations it takes to justify them, then equality of this sort is, to paraphrase the words of the U.S. Supreme Court, inherently inequitable. If the curriculum, for example, denigrates one's ancestors, religion, contributions to the history of the human race, and full dignity— that is, if it teaches the superiority of one segment of a democratic society over others—it is damaging to the minds and spirits of children, all children, those taught that their cultures are secondary and those given the false security of believing they are the creators of culture. An equitable curriculum must affirm all people as creators of culture and honor the multiplicity of human efforts to come to terms with living on earth.

It may seem that I am overstating the degree to which the myths of Western European culture are accepted as norms and imposed on children of other cultures. However, I want to cite a young people's geography book published by the prestigious house of Knopf, a subsidiary of Random House (Rosenthal, 1992). On page 84 of the book there is a comic strip entitled Europe. In the fifth panel Eastern Europe is referred to as "a jumble of cultures, languages and religions, and borders are still changing" where according to the author "Western Europe's borders have been stable for the past two hundred years." One has to wonder how much geohistory the author used in his research. I believe that in 1793 there was no Italy, Germany, or Austria. I also believe that there were a number of border changes in Western Europe after World War I, during the Third Reich, and in the last few years. It is hard to imagine where the authors came up with their simplification, though perhaps they too were victims of the myth of a stable, culturally and otherwise superior Western Europe. This guess is reinforced by the last panel, which shows a middle-class white couple looking at a neatly planned garden with plots labeled Sweden, France, Spain, Portugal, and so forth. The caption is "Europe, it is like a carefully tended garden." The man is saying, "Perhaps France could use some fertilizer," and the woman comments, "My, what a lovely Europe."

Tell that to the Catalans, Walloons, Irish, Scots, Welsh, northern Italians, and so on.

And look at page 38, which has a similar comic about South America. What does it say? Here's a sampler: "Home to many famous plants and animals," "The Amazon—world's oldest jungle," and "the fragile environment of the rain forest survives through cooperation." On the page there is only one human pictured, a man wearing a sombrero and serape who lives in the Patagonian desert and says, "Not so hot . . ." to which a stone responds, "Sez you." This is in contrast to the 19 people shown on the page devoted to Europe. No tended garden here.

I am frankly surprised that a publishing house as sophisticated as Knopf didn't pick up on the Eurocentrism and barely disguised racism represented by this geography. Maybe the schools are more effective than we have imagined in blinding us to the inequities and misrepresentations of monoculturalism.

The negative aspects of the kind of pseudo-history and geography presented as truth to children is damaging to people of European American descent as well as other people. It applies to Irish, Anglo, German, and Italian Americans, and to Jewish Americans like me. And the positive results of embracing multiculturalism can be felt by all of us too. I remember as child going to P.S. 104 in the late 1940s the elation our community felt when the Jewish High Holidays were made school holidays for every child in the New York City public schools. It meant that everyone acknowledged us; that if it was fair to have Christmas vacation then we were right in believing that it was also fair that everyone get off school to acknowledge the High Holy Days. The Jewish community had made a strong statement of its commitment to multiculturalism, one unfortunately repudiated by some members of the same community who now question the right of other cultures to have all children acknowledge their most precious cultural practices.

As a Jew who is intermarried and does not practice the religion or politics of any of the versions of Judaism in the United States, I still know that I am not of the so-called majority. I am often misunderstood because non-Jews assume they know what I believe and where my loyalties lie. They also assume that I am a stranger, not one of them. This became delightfully apparent to me one day when I was a visiting professor at a university in St. Paul, Minnesota. It was a freezing, windy, and chilling day. I was standing on the corner waiting to be picked up by a friend and one of the chaplains of the university came along. He passed me and I noticed him staring. I said "Hi," and he turned and said, "Why . . . why . . . you look absolutely Old Testament." My frizzy hair was blowing in the wind and indeed I looked absolutely Jewish to him, as if Jews have an absolute look. My father has blond hair and blue eyes. I told him thanks and was depressed for the next few days.

My depression was not much different from the depression of the parents and teachers I worked with in southern Texas. Its source was the sense that the people in power were ignorant and biased and that you had no way to let them know it. It also came from the fact that it wasn't fair that you had to be less than yourself to be part of a so-called democratic society. Or that your children would be punished simply for being who they were. In the context of schools, equity and multiculturalism are inextricable.

Multiculturalism is at the center of the struggle for fairness and decency, and depression is only a first response to inequity. Often it is followed by rage and then by organized dissent. The people I worked with in southern Texas got beyond their depression and as their first goal decided to persuade the current principal to leave. They chose two strategies. The first, which was used earlier by the United Bronx Parents and other advocates of community control of schools, was to create a report card to evaluate the principal. The report card was designed to resemble the actual report card children received quarterly at the school. However, it was bilingual. The categories to be graded ranged from "cooperates with parents," "has good working habits," "motivates student performance," "is effective in motivating staff to teach basic skills," "produces high test scores on a school wide bases," to "creates a school environment that respects the community." These categories were developed in a series of workshops conducted by parents and some community organizers.

The workshops themselves were extremely valuable as exercises in community self-education. It was the first time that uninhibited public debates about the schools had occurred in that community. It was a first step in the community having a voice in the education of its children.

The report cards were distributed and the results tallied. Then a summary of the principal's grades along with over 400 of the report cards were sent to the principal.

As a second strategy several unidentified members of the community decided to do a bit of creative multiculturalism. They took down the cutouts of Anglo children in the hall and replaced them with blowups of graduates of the school who had succeeded. The principal removed those posters not, according to him, because it was a bad idea, but because he did not give permission for it to be done.

At a public meeting the principal decided to assert his authority. He declared that parents would no longer be allowed in the building during school hours. Several community activists confronted him over this and he refused to respond to them since they weren't parents. So some parents took up the argument and after a while he called the meeting to an end. However, that wasn't the end of it. As people were leaving the building he was overheard talking to his assistant principal by several parents and activists: As I understand it, he said something to the effect that the parents were ignorant, uncivilized, and easily swayed by radicals. Moreover many of them were not good Christians and brought primitive beliefs such as voodoo from Mexico. At this he showed not merely his cultural and geographic ignorance but his fear of the community. For the next several weeks the principal received anonymous packages in the mail at home and at school. They contained strange-smelling powders and potions, chicken parts, cotton doused in what looked like blood, fingernail clippings. He called the police and they told him not to worry. He asked parents what all of this meant and got no response. After a while he couldn't sleep and felt uncomfortable walking through the halls at school by himself. A combination of this strategy and the receipt of the report cards convinced him to take early retirement. The principal's ignorance of the history, power, and curative effects of Santoria played a role in his retirement. It may be that he watched too many Western European and American movies about other people's cultures and believed in the constructions these films made to scare and amuse white audiences. In any case the community spoke both subtly and directly to him and showed them what they really felt about Eurocentric ways and his disrespect for their children. He was replaced by a Mexican-American principal. Though problems did not end, a step toward greater equity had been taken.

These are not strategies I'd necessarily recommend. But they do illustrate how ignorance pervades monocultural thinking and by implication the curriculum that embodies it. And it shows how silly and ingenious we sometimes have to be in the service of our children and their dignity. This is a sad commentary on how far we are from being a society that has high regard for equity, though it is encouraging to know that occasionally

the antic spirit emerges triumphant in the struggle for multiculturalism and plain and ordinary fairness.

However, it is important to go beyond mere harassment and
defensive struggle. There are many different forms that the
struggle for equity can take. One is to write about it as Derrick
Bell does. To paraphrase the title of Ishmael Reed's (1991) recent
book of essays, writing is a form of fighting and people tend to
forget that. To create new narratives and tell tales that move
people to action is no small thing. However, to do that you have
to find an audience and a way to reach them. Bell (1989, 1992)
in particular has managed to reach out through the popular
media to create a more honest critical discussion of race as an
abiding problem in the United States. He has been bold enough
to propose that racism is so much a part of the psyche in our
society that it will never go away and that therefore struggles
for equity will never end. This has led to considerable debate
about his relationship to Black Nationalism and the Nation of
Islam, all of which is for the good. Critical discussion of sensitive issues is usually so sanitized in the popular media that the
presence of an intelligent and strident voice like Bell's provides
a healthy irritant to a comatose public.

Another way to use the intellect and writing in the service of
equity is to reconstruct the curriculum and demystify what I
call the "excellence demagogues." These are the experts who
claim that quality and excellence is their territory and that
multiculturalism is at best a secondary enrichment of the curriculum and at worst a dilution of the substance of education
for all children. They would substitute historical misrepresen-
tation, cultural chauvinism, and the poverty of majoritarian
narrative for the richness of multicultural learning. A somewhat sophisticated example of this attitude was a proclamation
printed in large type across the front of a pamphlet for a seminar
on the arts in the schools that a former graduate student of mine
sent me recently: "We need to study Western Cultures to understand our past. We need to study non-Western cultures to
understand our future" (Boyer, 1993).

This quote, attributed to Ernest Boyer of the Carnegie Foundation for the Advancement for Teaching, reminds me of another quote I found on a post card in London a few years ago:

Reporter: "Mr. Gandhi: what do you think of Western Civilization?"

Gandhi: I think it would be a good idea.

The covert message of Boyer's quote might be loosely paraphrased in the following way:

We, the white Americans, need to study a romanticized version of Western European cultures such as Germany, France, and England, excepting most of the Mediterranean countries and East Europe other than where and when they fit into our notion of the Glory that was Greece and Splendor that was Rome, but not including contemporary Italy and Greece. The reason for this is to understand the superior values built into these interpretations of our white presumed past and to continue to fight for our dominance over the rest of the world. We also need to study non-Western and especially Asian cultures to understand our future as they are getting too powerful for their own good and we will have to confront them about this in the future.

Gandhi's message needs no paraphrasing.

The norming of excellence is standard form in the schools and usually goes unnoticed. One battle we must all fight is the reconstruction of the content of learning and the redefinition of excellence. This means that the notion of excellence will not be based on the premises of any one culture but tied to the quality of work within a multiplicity of traditions. We must find a way to help children see our collective history from many perspectives and understand that oppression does not provide the same experience for the oppressed as it does for the oppressor. We must also open children to the wonder of difference and help them come to terms with the genius of all peoples as well as become intimate with the finest and most illuminating products of those imaginations.

Teachers do not have to do this by themselves, though we must become students again and learn to teach in new ways and new perspectives what we thought we knew. There are scholars in many fields of study who are constructing multiple narratives and creating new vocabularies and understandings. In the case of the literature of African and African-American people we have to read people like Henry Louis Gates, Jr., and integrate into our daily life his insights and those of his colleagues. Gates (1986) describes, in the context of the literature of black people, what I am talking about for the literatures of the world and for learning in general:

> To theorize about black literatures, we must do what all theorists do. And that is to read the texts that comprise our literary tradition, formulate (by reasoning from observed facts) useful principles of criticism from within that textual tradition, then draw upon these to read the texts that make up that tradition. . . . My position is that for a critic of black literature to borrow European or American theories of literature regardless of "where they come from" is for that critic to be trapped in a relation of intellectual indenture or colonialism . One must *know* one's textual terrain before it can be explored; one must know one's literary tradition before it can be theorized about. . . . To discourage us from reading our own texts in ways suggested by those very texts is to encourage new forms of neocolonialism. To attempt such readings is neither to suggest that "black" texts have no "white" antecedents nor that the Western literary and critical traditions have no relevance for critics of "other" literatures. (p. 406)

In words that speak more directly to teachers of young children, we must enter other worlds of literature, imagination, and culture to enrich ourselves and inform our teaching. This enrichment is at the heart of excellence and is the core of equity. The two cannot be separated, and as hard as it is to relearn what we thought we knew there is no other responsible choice.

References

Ayers, W. (1989). *The good preschool teacher.* New York: Teachers College Press.

Bell, D. (1989). *And we are not saved: The elusive quest for racial justice.* New York: Basic Books.

Bell, D. (1992). *Faces at the bottom of the well: The permanence of racism.* New York: Basic Books.

Boyer, E. (1993). *Human commonalities reshaping the core.* Speech presented at the 12th Annual Conference of the Community College General Education Association, Lowell, MA.

Christian, B. (1985). *Black feminist criticism.* New York: Arno Press.

Coles, R. (1986). *The political life of children.* Boston: Atlantic Monthly Press.

DuBois, W. E. B. (1925). *Crisis, 40.*

Gates, H. L., Jr. (Ed.). (1986). *"Race" writing and difference.* Chicago: University of Chicago Press.

Hamilton, V. (1989). *The people could fly.* New York: Knopf.

Pignatelli, F., & Pflaum, S. (Eds.). (1992). *Celebrating diverse voices: Progressive education and equity.* Newbury Park, CA: Corwin.

Pintner, R. (1924). *Intelligence testing: Methods and results.* New York: Henry Holt.

Reed, I. (1991). *Writin' is fightin'.* New York: Macmillan.

Ringgold, F. (1991). *Tar Beach.* New York: Crown.

Rosenthal, P. (1992). *Everywhere on earth: A geografunny guide to the globe.* New York: Knopf.

Synnott, M. G. (1979). The admission and arsenal of minority students at Harvard, Yale and Princeton 1900-1950. *History of Education Quarterly, 19*(3), 289.

Washinton, J. M. (Ed.). (1992). *I have a dream: Writing and speeches that changed the world.* Washington, DC: Harper.

10. Shifting the Paradigm: You Must Have a Dream to Build a School

HERB ROSENFELD

Some 30-odd new secondary schools will open in New York City during the next 2 years. Each of these schools will depart to some extent from the traditional secondary school model. These schools will feature a variety of schoolwide curriculum themes and organizational structures.

What kind of experience awaits the founders of those schools generated from the notion of equity-based education? An equity-based education nurtures the strengths of each student with equal fervor and provides an atmosphere that enables each student to use increasingly developed strengths to buttress their entire education experience.

In this chapter I relate some of the details of the creation of the East Side Community High School, a school driven by educational equity. This story will be of particular interest to those who ponder the question, "Can we create schools that value students at all achievement levels, not just the gifted ones?"

The teachers and others involved in the development of this school insist that students labeled "at risk," or those students who would normally drop out of school, can and should become active learners and productive citizens. In addition, they believe it is the school's responsibility to configure itself to support this outcome.

In designing this school, the staff pursued a process that involved peeling back the layers of traditional schools (where the labels of student failure originated). At the same time, they synthesized innovative educational components into a highly personalized climate, forming a very different kind of public secondary school. Although the staff has had considerable success, it is from their trials and tribulations we learn most about transforming schools or building new ones dedicated to the concept of educational equity.

Building the Dream

The decision to explore the development of a new secondary school was made in spring 1991 in a meeting with William Ubiñas, the Superintendent of Community School, at which we discussed school change in general and the kind of work being done by the restructuring movement in particular.

Ubiñas, who had done research with Sizer (in the study that produced *Horace's Compromise*, 1984), was greatly concerned with the large number of young men and women (overwhelmingly minority) who wound up on the streets of the Lower East Side of Manhattan rather than in school. With that in mind and influenced by his experience with Sizer, he had been considering the idea of creating a secondary school (grades 7-12) in his district. He wanted this school to have a learner-centered environment, focusing on the immediate school community (i.e., District 1) as a living environment. The essential idea was to link student empowerment that would result from equity-based education with the students' acquisition of knowledge and understanding of their own world. He asked me if I would design, plan, and generally facilitate the establishment of such a school.

Ubiñas, his deputy Irma Zardoya, and I immediately began the preparation work necessary to get a new school started. By October 1991, through a series of information meetings, we gained the support of the District 1 Community School Board, and I then composed a rough draft of the school design for the board's approval. The board in turn authorized us to create a plan for the new school, which would open September 1992. Ubiñas formed a task force consisting of representatives from the high school division, the local school board, the district office, the district parents, the United Federation of Teachers, the Council of Supervisors and Administrators, a variety of community-based organizations, and some school-based District 1 personnel. Our intention was to create a broad base of support for our school.

We believed that through the process of cooperatively developing a school design, we could establish a good understanding of our school concept. This broad sketch was generated from the notion that every child can learn and realize his or her potential in the appropriate setting (i.e., one of educational equity). We identified this task force as our school network, which would later be replaced by the students, parents, and staff of the newly created school. We worked until May 1992 elaborating the rough draft we had presented to the District 1 board. The result was a concept paper consistent with contractual demands, the by-laws of the New York City Board of Education, and District I's mandate to Ubiñas. The final draft of the concept paper was the embodiment of our collective dream. It was the collaboratively composed framework from which the staff would actually create their school. This collectively constructed paper served as the blueprint for the East Side Community High School.

The Planning Process

We were then prepared to hire a director (Jill Herman), with whom I developed a mentoring relationship that has carried through the first year of the school's existence. Over the next 2 months we recruited students and hired the staff. The director played a pivotal role in leading the staff through the tasks that were to be done. The staff, working collaboratively, fleshed out the school organization, planned curriculum, ordered materials, and made all of the necessary preparations to open the school's doors and welcome 80 seventh-grade students to the East Side Community High School in September 1992.

The first planning problem we faced was to develop simple, clear educational standards that would be acceptable to the entire school network (i.e., *every member* of our task force) and that would be generated from our conception of educational equity. Consequently, we designed the school blueprint by planning backward. That is, we first established a mission statement (derived from our concept paper), then decided what our student exit outcomes would be. Recognizing these outcomes as our standards, we then developed a school structure reflecting these standards.

In the development of this framework, we drew largely on the work some of us had done with the Coalition of Essential Schools. We also looked to some of the open-classroom, learner-centered elementary schools that have emerged in New York City over the last 20 years and studied their curriculum development, classroom practices, and student expectations. As a result, the school we set out to build was to have the following characteristics:

- It would be small, no more than 480 students in Grades 7 through 12.
- Curriculum would be integrated, project driven, and organized around themes and strands.
- The staff would work collaboratively on curriculum development.
- The climate would be highly personalized and nonviolent.
- Learning would be of paramount importance and would be interactive.
- Graduation would include student portfolio requirements.
- Student assessment would be designed to support individualization and enhance the student learning experience.

It was difficult to draw from the personal experience of the staff, because the traditional secondary schools they came from were mostly concerned with the efficient delivery of lower order thinking skills and an establishment of an extensive information data base. Traditional schools are organized accordingly, featuring:

- Short classes 40-45 minutes long

- Strictly discrete academic disciplines
- Textbook-based curriculum
- Tracked classes with population determined by scores on standardized examinations
- Assessment by pen-and-pencil, often short-answer examinations
- Graduation by Carnegie units

In stark contrast to these features, the Coalition speaks to the *whole child* and *each individual child*. Open-classroom teachers acknowledge and pay tribute to the many and wonderful differences in children, and so we looked to their way of working with students and parents to inform our own practices.

Consequently, unlike planners in traditional high schools, who look to the university classroom for pedagogical excellence, we saw the creative kindergarten as our inspiration. The mental image and the dream depicted by this image was a place where children came to work, to learn, and of course, to grow, their bright faces and clear minds ready to puzzle though the dilemmas of, for example, Marie Curie and James Baldwin regardless of their class, gender, race, or test scores. Out of this experience would come their personal growth and empowerment as citizens of a democratic society, who have the will and the ability to reach for their own personal fulfillment.

Learner-Centered Environments

How do these model kindergartens work? What could we find for ourselves in their "learner-centered" ideas?

First of all, similar to their elementary school colleagues everywhere, each open-classroom teacher is responsible for the education of 30-some students (unlike secondary school teachers who see about 150 students a day). Open-classroom teachers interpret their responsibility to mean that they must develop an empathy for and insight into:

- The way that each of their students understands the world around her or him

- How their students process information
- What the mathematical, scientific, and historical models of the world mean to their students
- How much and what kind of knowledge their students bring to school

To separately address the learning needs of each student, each person working with these students is required to have a powerful respect for diversity and an affirmative, positive reaction to inquiry. Further, to better understand these needs, these teachers find it invaluable to develop a positive and supportive working relationship with parents. This is accomplished as parents find a meaningful role in their child's learning experiences. For example, parents and teachers working together consider questions like:

- Is the television distracting?
- Is it worthwhile to read newspapers?
- Which computer games lead to the construction of information and strategy building?
- Is there a connection between the way people interact at home and the way that students function in the school?
- What are the advantages of deliberately nonviolent behavior?

Much of the working through of these issues is done at family conferences and through very frequent telephone conversations.

Teachers come to know how students make sense of the world by assigning them in-class activities for which strategy building and the use of prior knowledge are demanded. One may also develop assessment instruments requiring students to expose and demonstrate their way of thinking, reasoning, and working. It is therefore necessary to create a classroom atmosphere where it is possible for the teacher to work along with each student on a daily basis over a long period of time, a process not possible in the typical secondary school class, where the students are neatly seated in rows, facing forward, listening to the teacher hold forth at the blackboard or at her or his desk.

We felt that for the East Side School to achieve this degree of personalization, we would have to drastically reduce both class size and the total number of students each teacher sees on a daily basis. How could we possibly accomplish this with our present level of funding? We needed more teachers and fewer students, but because our funding was limited, what we considered to be a necessary condition for educational equity seemed insurmountable. But this dilemma led us to examine the ideas of integrated curriculum, which were very consistent with the way our elementary school models worked with children and would allow for the kind of restructuring of workloads we needed to pursue.

Integrated Curriculum

In trying to develop a way to have students use their strengths to support their deficits, the experiences of teachers in learner-centered environments suggest they could learn most about their students when they are working on long-term projects. As they work from the planning stage through the final product, students have special opportunities to discover and display skills normally ignored in tracked situations where manipulative skills and information-intensive curricula are emphasized. Long-term projects are often stimulated by the analysis and synthesis of information and strategies from two or more different academic disciplines. For example, in one class that I know of, students were asked to design and build a playground model for the school campus to be used after school hours by community members for social as well as sporting events. The work of school science, social studies, art, computer science, and mathematics were all included in such a project.

We also believed that multiage, heterogeneously grouped classes would be an important part of the student learning gestalt at the East Side Community School. But because high schools are traditionally bastions of specialization, how could we ever translate this idea so that it would work on a high school level? And even if we could, where could we get the classroom materials needed to orient students to the kind of thinking required in these cross-curriculum, integrated projects? We clearly had to look at "subject matter" differently from the way we were used to looking at it. Our solution was to order ideas and information by strands and themes instead of units and topics, a technique long employed by progressive elementary educators. And so we focused on themes like power, justice, growth, measure, transportation, communication, energy, counting, motion, revolution, and so on for curriculum design.

To broaden specialist teachers' ability to create everyday activities for the students and development assessment instruments, we worked in teams. This process generated new problems of its own. We found when teachers plan from scratch, they have to have a deeper understanding of their curricular specialty, so they can coordinate with their planning partners. In addition, because they were integrating across disciplines, they often had to find their ideas in themes and projects that appeared to emphasize one discipline over another. For example, a mathematics teacher who has learned to think of mathematics as a collection of equations and geometric figures might have to find the mathematical thinking embedded in the argument that defends or opposes the political decision to enforce "AIDS testing for public service personnel"; or she might have to work with students who are trying to determine "the cost for each American of the cleanup of the Exxon spill in Alaska." Such projects seem less complex from the "social studies" vantage point because good social studies teachers are used to researching and developing arguments supporting a point of view and writing about them, whereas good mathematics teachers are used to finding the solutions to problems that may easily be reduced to algebraic equations or simple geometric propositions. But a closer look reveals a problem that often arises for social studies teachers. They are not used to supporting their arguments with the sophisticated estimation or counting strategies, as well as graphs, data charts, and probabilistic arguments that these projects call for. Yes, collaboration and curriculum integration are huge issues that grow and grow as the students' work becomes more sophisticated. All of this, just to institute heterogeneous grouping!

Pedagogy

While grappling with the above dilemmas, it became clear that we also would have to take a good look at the way we ran our classes. We knew that learner-centered classes were usually rather informal, with students working alone or in small groups in various parts of the learning space. The students would be actively engaged in their own learning, talking, arguing, modeling, and so forth. What in the world would be the shape, the look, the feel of our secondary school classrooms? The consideration of the following questions greatly informed our decisions on the ways we would shape our seminar and workshop-type classes. They also highlight our ongoing staff development needs:

- Will 7th-grade students, already molded in the traditional hierarchical school mode be able to handle this kind of informality? Will the staff?
- What will happen in the class? Will there be developmental type lessons?
- If not, what will students do in classes? What will teachers do?
- Will students be seated in the traditional formation?
- What kind of furniture will we need? Some of our elementary school colleagues have rugs and couches in their classrooms!
- How will technology fit in?
- What would be the new standard for a good class? A good group of classes?
- How should students comport themselves? Should visitors be welcome in the classes? How about parents? How about colleagues?
- How can colleagues best support each other?
- What are the new responsibilities of the students? What about parents?
- What is the new role of the teachers?

The Teachers' New Roles

Clearly our teachers would have to assume a different role. Rather than the teacher being the center of the classroom, the students would become the center. A good class would be one in which the teacher seldom held forth. Whole-group discussion would become more of a sharing in which students raised more and more probing questions and proposed avenues of research for appropriate problem-solving strategies as coping mechanisms.

For us, the day of the virtuoso teacher is over. Although our graduates might still most fondly remember a favorite adviser or teacher, teachers would be revered and acclaimed for their patience rather than their charisma; for their encouragement rather than their delivery; for their willingness to listen, to question, to guide and their respect for the opinions of students, rather than their encyclopedic knowledge. All of this while keeping in mind that erudition was to remain highly treasured. We also felt it important to keep in mind that the way the staff worked would influence the students. Consequently, if we think it vital for students to learn to collaborate, we have to examine our own way of working together.

Collaboration and Equity

It is especially true if each segment of the school community is to be empowered, that all of the relationships within the school would differ from the typical. Our school leadership had to take on the issues of curriculum, pedagogy, working with parents and climate setting rather than focusing solely on organization management. To collaborate our teachers found they needed more support from each other. Our students have to be much more self-reliant, and their parents must be more finely tuned to what their children are experiencing in school. These roles, of course, are very new for traditional secondary school people and created a very different school climate. In the lexicon of equity, the words respect and trust become the most meaningful descriptors of what we all learned to expect from each other. Staff deliberations at each of our planning sessions, whether dealing with curriculum, pedagogy, student staffing, school policy, or school governance, were driven by the following set of questions:

- Will it provide and support multicultural experiences?
- How will parents respond?
- Will others in the school community understand what we are trying to accomplish?

It is this complexity of questions and the issues they imply that dominated much of the thinking and planning for the staff in the first months of East Side's existence and still motivates it.

Scheduling, Governance, and Collaboration

After considering curriculum, classroom practices, staff collaboration, and school climate in our school planning, the last pieces remaining to the school puzzle (or more appropriately domino board) were the daily class schedule and the school governance arrangements. The class schedule has to satisfy the work needs of the students, who now would be spending most of their time in class working alone or with others on ongoing projects, searching out materials in the library, and making field trips. In addition, the schedule would have to facilitate the teaching of integrated curricula as well as provide for in-school planning time for the curriculum teams. Similarly, to reduce our maximum class size from 34 to 20 students, we determined the teaching staff would have to be creatively deployed. We found we could satisfy all of these conditions by adopting a block programming schedule with longer, but fewer classes each day. This was made possible through the integration of two or more curricula into one (e.g., math/science, humanities) and the use of teachers as generalists rather than as specialists.

At the same time, the development of school policy and the establishment of a workable and democratic decision-making mechanism required that we create an atmosphere in which each constituency in the school community felt legitimately empowered and could assume a meaningful responsibility for the school as a whole while pressing for their own particular operational needs. In addition, student individualization dictates that all staff members assume a meaningful responsibility for the education of each student as a *whole human being,* and therefore they must have a global understanding of the school community. The governance system is in its infancy and is growing and changing even as I write.

The sense of community resulting from this way of governing the school brings to mind the African proverb, "It takes a whole village to raise a child." A reasonable American analogue might be that it takes a whole school community to properly educate a child.

It also takes time for the staff to develop a way of working that enables the school to keep growing and changing consistent with the essence of educational equity. The students, parents, and staff are the working parts of this ongoing process, each with their own roles and conscious of the roles of their partners. Each of these spokes must undertake continuous self-appraisal with the help and support of the other spokes for this wheel to keep rolling forward. This is where honesty becomes most important and is most difficult. Honesty is an essential feature of a meaningful self-appraisal process. A school's staff cannot move on without constantly examining its own professional practices, and this is a process that requires a healthy interdependence.

Summary

What follows are the fundamental "nuggets of need" I gleaned from my experience with East Side:

- Whether starting a new school or rethinking an existing one, the designers of a school must have a dream. The dream must be understood and embraced by the entire school community and by the organizational network of which the school is a part.

- The fundamental school concept might come from any segment of the community (teachers, school administration, superintendent, school board, parents), but the development of the school's mission must include representatives from all stakeholders of that community.
- The mission should focus on *student outcomes.* The school climate, curriculum classroom practices, and adult organization should be designed with the fulfillment of these outcomes (which are appropriate standards of good school practices) in mind.
- True school change takes time, patience, persistence, and the willingness to *honestly* examine one's own work. It often requires an objective but understanding outsider to work with the school staff.
- The operant behavior descriptors of an equity-based school are *respect, trust,* and *honesty.*
- Professional development for both the leadership and the teaching staff should be ongoing and is crucial. *Most of the work is on developing and maintaining a different understanding of school.*

All of the above becomes most difficult when the bedrock idea that generates the dream is educational equity. This is particularly true because it becomes necessary to dismantle and replace virtually all of the familiar school structures. And while these changes are taking place, school still must be carried on in a meaningful way.

Even those school people who are critical of their own school practices often have great difficulty conceiving of a school without some of its more familiar forms, like bell schedules, sequentialized textbook-driven curriculum, classes controlled by parliamentary procedure, and student assessment by in-class short-answer tests. It requires great conviction and dedication to facilitate change and to be able to maintain and defend innovative measures, even as unexpected obstacles present a greater challenge.

Reference

Sizer, T. (1984). *Horace's compromise.* Boston: Houghton Miflin.

11. "Did You Notice That They Didn't Eat?" Power and Culture in Ethnographic Evaluation Research

NANCY BARNES

In this chapter, I explore the possibilities and dilemmas facing ethnographic researchers who seek to support progressive reforms in public education in the 1990s. Partisan research sounds like an oxymoron; I believe, however, that partisan, or positioned ethnography is the way we must think about research that can be genuinely useful to teachers, administrators, and communities working to improve their schools. I want to pull apart the strands of what it means to do explicitly positioned studies that are concerned with equity issues not only in the schools but also in the doing of research itself. Specifically, I want to ask whether evaluation—a form of research that schools are often compelled to accept—can be fair and respectful of practitioners who are struggling for change on an everyday basis.

I have come to these concerns through my participation in an ethnographic evaluation of what I will call the "neighborhood school program" (NSP), at one public elementary school, P.S. Y. Neighborhood schools represent an effort to expand the resources of schools in poor, or as the bureaucrats sometimes say, "intensely distressed" neighborhoods. The idea is to incorporate extended-day and summer activities, to offer programs for parents, and to coordinate social services and health care at the school site, thus drawing community-based organizations and other outside resources into the life of the school.

Public directives about the NSP list "academic improvement" among the program's highest goals. The evaluation I worked on called in parallel fashion for academic outcomes to be examined during the study. This assumption, to which I will return, became increasingly problematic for me during the months I functioned as a member of the evaluation team.

P.S. Y is besieged by the interlocking problems of poverty, drugs, AIDS, violence, and inadequate social services in a community suffering as intensely as any in New York City. The school has been academically weak, as measured by citywide standardized tests, for some time. In recent years a dynamic principal has developed the school into a haven of personal safety and cultural supports for the children of this community.

The research involved observations of the daily activities at the school, as well as tracking and documentation of various aspects of the new programs as the NSP developed at selected school sites. Before the project began, I had understood that school evaluation is an inescapably normative and political activity, particularly in relation to poor children and children in the African American and Latino communities. I had less sense of the strain that evaluation places on school staff and the layered obligations it involves. Practitioners tend to be incredibly busy, more so if a school is facing major obstacles or restructuring. Both of these were the case at P.S. Y. The study I worked on was funded by a private foundation, which added yet another ambiguous layer of accountability as the NSP was created by the state's education bureaucracy.

The experience at P.S. Y was my first venture into the highly complex world of contracted research in public education. I am a cultural anthropologist with an abiding ambivalence about the political and ethical questions raised by social science research; the experience at P.S. Y has been as troubling as it has been instructive to me. I am left grappling with questions about whether research can ever truly support the efforts at change and fairness that are fundamental to the current school reform movement, and with whether evaluation itself can possibly become a more equitable process.

Perhaps the dilemmas I encountered reflect my intellectual training as an anthropologist. My time as a participant observer at P.S. Y was marked by at least two characteristic dimensions of anthropological fieldwork: observing and collecting data at the school, and observing (and collecting data on) the research itself, which included me. It is from this reflexive starting point that I want to develop my argument for "positioned ethnography," a consciousness with which to articulate strategies for research that can serve the interests of progressive school change.

Program evaluations almost always concern money and power and other, only slightly more subtle forms of legitimation and resource distribution. That is true here, in that the fate of the NSP pilot project may determine future support for neighborhood schools. The role of an ethnographic evaluator thus raises critical questions at every stage of the research process: assembling data, understanding that it presents multiple interpretations both inside and outside the school, brokering those understandings as an analysis is generated.

What power does the school have in a situation like this? What is the role of the foundation or other third party that funds the evaluation and pays the ethnographer? These are crucial questions for research that is to be useful to those who are studied or for evaluations that reflect equity and respect for school practitioners. Rather than untangle the sticky web of evaluation research, I will approach the questions somewhat obliquely. I want to imagine a "positioned ethnography" that makes conscious and visible the complex power relations implicit in such situations. Pioneering evaluation studies are now being conceived and designed as collaborative and even participatory projects. Here, however, I explore questions that arose in the course of a rather ordinary evaluation project.

Events in the Field

The story I tell here is about a crisis that occurred during my fieldwork. It concerns my effort, first, to name the politically troubling issues that emerged in the course of the evaluation, and then, to grasp why nobody wanted to address them. Even as events were happening, I suspected that the dimensions of fairness, power, and culture I was grappling with were hardly unique to this project.

Toward the end of the first year of the research, the evaluation team produced a draft of a report on the neighborhood school program. The draft was intended as a working document, to be read only by a restricted group of individuals in the research and foundation worlds. It was definitely *not* intended for the people in the neighborhood schools. The draft of the report was, however, handed around in the schools. No one was quite sure how this happened; my own feeling is that it happened because the cultural borders between public schools, state and city education bureaucrats, private foundations, and the consultants who roam back and forth across these boundaries are more porous than we realize. Certainly more of us have multiple identities in this world than we customarily acknowledge.

In any case, the report's distribution wreaked havoc at P.S. Y. The distress and betrayal that people felt came from the event, the fact that it happened, more than from the content of the report. The event undermined relationships I had spent months establishing; it also raised deeply buried questions about research. Despite my professional obligations to the people who hired me, I realized that I needed new tools and concepts with which to imagine doing ethnographic evaluation that I could personally support.

My search for new ways of thinking has been influenced by a stream of relatively new work in interpretive and critical anthropology. Renato Rosaldo's *Culture and Truth* (1989) will have to serve as one important voice from this rich and politically sensitive conversation. As the ethnographic evaluator at the neighborhood school I embodied what Rosaldo (1989) calls the "positioned subject":

> The ethnographer, as a positioned subject, grasps certain human phenomena better than others. He or she occupies a position or structural location and observes with a particular angle of vision. Consider for example how age, gender, being an outsider, and association with a neocolonial regime influence what the ethnographer learns. The notion of position also refers to how life experiences both enable and inhibit particular kinds of insight. (p. 19)

The experience at P.S. Y further demonstrates that not only do individuals bring angles of vision that significantly influence their research, as Rosaldo suggests, but a research venture itself, both in its general context, such as educational research, and in the particulars of each project, entails "positions" that must be scrutinized.

Let me continue the story drawn from my field notes so as to explore how Rosaldo's idea of position permits new ways of thinking about ethnographic research in schools. Following the inadvertent circulation of the draft report, everyone at P.S. Y was talking about what an outrage it was that they had not been consulted. Whenever I entered a room or joined a discussion, silence fell. Within a couple of days, I figured out that members of the school staff had indeed read the report, even though it was not officially shown to anyone. (I had not yet seen the report myself, although it was based on my observations along with data supplied from other schools in the NSP.)

The ethnographer (I) endeavored to convince the evaluators (watch how my language already separates me from them, even though I was a member of the team) that if this was indeed a formative evaluation as they claimed, then of course we ought to be talking about it with the school practitioners. Their resistance took the form of simply not grasping why this might be helpful.

Eventually, a meeting of all the important players in the NSP was called. The players included the two bilingual Puerto Rican women who effectively run the school, the principal and the coordinator of the neighborhood school project (herself a former evaluator); the man who directs the evaluation; and the woman who directs the foundation that supports it. These two, like me, are both white Ph.D.s. Besides me, the final member of the gathering was a master teacher, a white, male, native English speaker, relieved of classroom duties to perform administrative tasks including the skilled manipulation of funded programs such as the NSP, on which the school depends. He was present because he is loyal to the principal's vision of the school, yet crosses cultural borders with ease.

Most of the meeting was devoted to exchanges about the circumstances surrounding the disastrous circulation of the draft of the evaluation report. The exchanges about this event were angry and defensive in turn; I will not reconstruct them here. The Latina leaders of the school appeared both vulnerable and angry, yet were virtually unable to ask direct, challenging questions about why the report had been passed around, much less what it said. The white evaluators were uncomfortable and guarded, consistently addressing their remarks to the white male teacher. They seemed vastly relieved at his presence, as he knows the rules of the discourse within which nobody would dream of asking difficult questions of the evaluators or the funders. The evaluation director's remarks indicated that he believed he had the best interests of the school at heart. It was unfortunate that this misunderstanding had occurred, since the report need not concern the practitioners at P.S. Y—but of course they were welcome to read it. The talk continued for more than an hour; none of it addressed substantive questions about the evaluation or the status of the NSP. Finally all who did not work in the school building left.

This messy, unresolved event weakened P.S. Y's already tentative reception of the evaluation; it also threatened my identity as participant observer. Even though a few individuals had a few embarrassing moments, the event did no damage outside the school. Significantly, the conceptual design of the evaluation was untouched, either by the meeting or by the crisis that had prompted it.

One distinctive characteristic of ethnographic inquiry is its insistence on the meanings that people themselves ("the natives") have of the issue at hand. But who *are* the natives? Who is indigenous in an elementary school that I visit in the city where I grew up? Why would this principal, for example, ever choose to become an informant in our study? Once again, I found myself overwhelmed by the need for new ways to think about what was happening.

The concept of position offers a start. The field notes distilled from the meeting depict elaborate multiple positions and multiple realities. At the time, I was left struggling with formidable complexities. To wit: I learned the principal's reaction several days later when she and I talked about the meeting. "Did you *notice*," she said to me, "did you notice that they didn't eat?"

The meeting fiasco had taken place in her office, and as is her custom, she had served a delicious fancy lunch of Latin dishes prepared by several parents who run a catering business, gotten off the ground partly by the NSP. "You know I always serve food when I have visitors to my school—*you* ate! This is just the same as when I have visitors in my home, and I just don't believe that they didn't even eat!"

That is exactly the system of meaning from which the principal also told me that she "spoke from the heart" in the meeting, that in fact everything she does regarding her school is from the heart. She simply could not grasp that the evaluation director had excused the circulation of the draft report by saying that it was not a public document.

To the director, his remark meant that although it was regrettable that the report had circulated prematurely, it didn't really matter because he did not plan to submit this document to the state. To her, it meant that a white man in a suit, someone in a position of power who makes recommendations that may affect what she wants to do at her school, was lying to her—who speaks from the heart.

It was good that I ate. But it took months to repair the damage done to my working relations at P.S. Y. Nothing changed in the formal arrangements or the informal understandings between the school and the evaluators. My attempts to heighten the dilemmas raised by the circulation of a report that had not been discussed with the school practitioners met with little response among the evaluators. The entire episode seems to raise issues of equity in research that are just as pressing as how the program spends its money or who makes decisions.

Ethnographers, Culture, and Power

What does the meeting fiasco reveal? What does this field-work story mean? Beyond the inconvenience it caused me, and the methodological issues it raises for others engaged in qualitative research, who cares? Recognizing "positioned research" permits me to rethink my stance as an ethnographic evaluator. The research strategies one can use to tackle these questions rest on the foundation of a bigger critical and reflexive tradition in social thought, which Simon and Dippo (1986) describe in this fashion, "to actually do ethnography is to engage in the process of knowledge production. . . . We must come to grips with the recognition that *most ethnographic data is 'produced' and not 'found' "*(p. 387, italics added).

I had, in other words, to excavate and explicate the dimensions of that ridiculous meeting precisely *because* ethnography—my work at the school—was itself "producing knowledge."

The use of ethnographic methods in educational research has become widespread and rather faddish in recent years. The borrowing, however, requires more than technique. It demands attention to the concepts with which ethnographies are produced as well, concepts like position, culture, interpretation. Those of us concerned with equity and progressive change when we enter schools as evaluators must learn to position ethnographic interpretations; we must also begin to investigate relations of power that implicate and involve the research and the researchers as well as the school community.

The ethnographer (I) certainly was "positioned" at the infamous meeting, as were the others described. In a sense, I represented precisely the possibilities and the dilemmas for this work that I am investigating here. The relations of power (one dimension of position) that were represented around the table in the principal's office, and in the neighborhood school project as a whole, rest on a particular axis. Rosaldo (1989) illuminates that axis with a concept I will call "studying difference," a shorthand label for a complex, nuanced thought.

To speak of studying difference emphasizes the delicately intertwined relations between culture and power. The evaluator's own relation to power is a sometimes troubling aspect of research at a school site. The fieldwork scene above needs to be framed by another quote from *Culture and Truth,* which addresses the politically laden balancing act that difference always bespeaks:

> In practice, the emphasis on difference results in a peculiar ratio: as the "other" becomes more culturally visible, the "self" becomes correspondingly less so. Social analysts, for example, often assert that subordinate groups have an authentic culture at the same time that they mock their own upper-middle-class professional culture. . . . Yet analysts rarely allow the ratio of class and culture to include power. Thus they conceal the ratio's darker side: the more power one has, the less culture one enjoys, and the more culture one has, the less power one wields. If "they'"have an explicit monopoly on authentic culture, "we" have an unspoken one on institutional power. (Rosaldo, 1989, p. 202)

This peculiar ratio *is* the reality in schools in a city like New York. Yet it is seldom noticed ("Did you *notice* that they didn't eat?") and almost never woven into ethnographic evaluation texts. The intricate relationships involved in studying difference are signposts marking the extent to which schools and researchers inexorably construct each other as the "other." This too becomes something to be documented and interpreted.

Concretely, how can "position" and "studying difference" frame qualitative research? What exactly changes, and why does it matter? There are many ways in which poorly conceived or executed research can harm a school; they range from loss of funding or other material support to the creation of conflicts within a group of practitioners. Those being studied often have no say whatsoever in the shaping of an evaluation; this clearly is an equity issue.

For those of us who do this kind of research, the imbalance of power is what demands new analytic tools like "studying difference." What should I do when the ethnographic findings—which *I* have produced—might hurt the people I, positioned as I am, most want to support? At P.S. Y this means the people in the school community, who may be perceived to have relatively more "culture" because the school is so strongly linked to the Latino community from which the children come. What if damage results because the data is misinterpreted, or simply not comprehended by influential outsiders with relatively more "power?" Who determines what is deemed data? Whose knowledge is this, anyway?

I will examine one instance of how my own consciousness of the possibilities of ethnographic evaluation have changed as I think about power and culture in terms of "positioned research"; and a second example of how "studying difference" has shifted my analysis of what defines success for the NSP.

First, evaluation studies are inescapably political. In the case of the neighborhood school evaluation the "field" included the state bureaucracy, the evaluators, and the external funders who paid us. As the ethnographer, I frequently chose to focus on "culture" in the school. But the "power" of whoever is paying the ethnographer also "produces" data.

What anthropologists refer to as "studying up" thus requires studying the powers-that-be. To reframe a research problem in this manner suggests not only "studying up" or "writing up," but studying ourselves (ethnographers), and ourselves in a position (up) that is closer to those who really do have power than we anthropologists usually like to be (Burawoy, 1991; Nader, 1969). Would I be emphasizing the interpretation of culture and power so heavily, if I had not realized how important it was to eat the meal that day we met in the principal's office?

From this perspective, the nightmare meeting itself becomes data for the evaluation, just as much as observing a parents' meeting on retention or interviewing the school nurse. I have attempted to write the story from my field notes so as to reflect this perspective. Inevitably, contradictions appear. Power resides in the state, yet I am advocating partisan research that supports reformers who want to change the state's educational system. Despite the contradictions, "noticing" and analyzing detailed relations of power in a school scene *does* yield changed consciousness. As Freire theorizes about education at large, "the form of action men [*sic*] adopt is to a large extent a function of how they perceive themselves in the world" (Freire, 1968, p. 71). The process is vivid in a city as diverse as New York.

My second illustration of a new perspective in ethnographic evaluation research concerns how the neighborhood schools were to be judged, which could affect funding and other forms of support for the program in the future. Neither the state mandate for the program nor the design of the evaluation had established guidelines for how to assess academic improvement under the auspices of the NSP. The troubling question that emerged repeatedly during the months of the evaluation was: What constitutes "success" for the neighborhood schools?

Nothing in the planning of the NSP, or its evaluation, had articulated how additional resources or community involvement (e.g., a theater program provided by a neighborhood settlement house) might be linked to better teaching and learning. Nothing. It seemed blatantly unfair to assess the neighborhood school program on the basis of traditional academic measures. At P.S. Y, the result could only be to blame the school for its "failures" once again.

Neighborhood schools may not be a route to academic improvement as measured by standardized tests—or they may, over time, as some of Comer's (1980) work suggests in comparable settings. This is not to say that academic outcomes don't matter—they do. Rather, the definition of success unearths another equity issue if the outsiders, who have relatively more power, can simply assert that academic improvement is *the* critical indicator of success for the neighborhood schools. As the ethnographer, positioned to hear community voices and appreciate the points of view of people who have relatively more culture, I had to challenge these assumptions.

Success for the neighborhood school program at P.S. Y might be indicated, alternatively, by the tremendous welcome extended to parents, many of whom are recent immigrants, or by the school's pervasive bilingualism, or the safe haven it represents on a block in a part of the city where adults as much as children live under siege from drugs and violence. My point is that those with power simply did not recognize these characteristics of the neighborhood school as elements of its success. This kind of blindness has broad consequences for policy making, just as the visiting evaluators' inability to acknowledge a problem when they had failed to consult about the draft report—or to eat—had consequences for the evaluation.

When theoretical frames like position and studying difference construct the ethnography, evaluation can be used to communicate to policy makers and funders how a strong and positive Latino identity (or culture, in the borderlands of poor neighborhoods in New York City) strengthens the children and the community. This marks a success for the neighborhood school program.

Perspectives on Ethnographic Research in Schools

What makes evaluation research worth doing is precisely the possibility of being positioned to produce data, and interpret it, and construct ethnographic accounts so that the enterprise becomes useful, whether that means protecting a school's female Latina leadership or brokering culture so that it is not subsumed by power. School restructuring and the highly politicized national debates on public education offer concrete openings for research that is overtly partisan, not in its findings but in its commitments, its position; research that names both the study of difference and the production of knowledge in its effort to encourage equity and support progressive reform. This is obviously easier said than done, as the fragment from my own fieldwork attests. I find myself searching for practical guidelines for participation in evaluation research, guidelines that also support progressive school change. Thus far, I can only offer three perspectives or vantage points from which to consider ethnographic research in schools.

First, we need to privilege the concept of position, to speak and write and reflect on our own positions as ethnographers throughout the process of the research. This may mean my personal and professional position, the circumstances and conditions of my life and thought. It also means the position of a given research project, which I have illustrated in terms of the evaluation of the NSP.

However elaborate it may seem, it is critical to pay close attention to position and context at all stages: before the study begins; as the ethnographer contracts to work for money, enters the field, or passes the security guard's desk in the school; up to and including the presentation of the data. In the situation of the misguided draft report, named allegiances or partisanship might have freed the research from some of the problems of what Fetterman (1984) calls "guilty knowledge and dirty hands" (p. 211).

To be aware of position is always a fluid, changeable consciousness because position is such a deeply contextual concept; its meanings shift continually. P.S. Y, for example, is populated with children from Thailand, Vietnam, Jamaica, Haiti, and a long list of countries in Latin America. Clearly, these children and their families are crossing many, many cultural boundaries. It may be less apparent that I too am crossing borders, whether as an anthropologist working at home, as a longtime college teacher learning to observe the classrooms of little children, or as a skeptical participant in an evaluation study intended to influence a state bureaucracy. Any of these details of position, or my beliefs about them, might be pertinent. Throughout, I have to acknowledge that I am producing knowledge, no matter how pretentious that sounds, rather than finding data.

The second perspective points me toward the delicate relations between what Rosaldo (1989) calls culture and power, especially in city schools structured by countless forms of diversity and inequality. When I arrived to begin observing at P.S. Y, for instance, they did not even know my name, much less have a chance to decide whether they wanted me there or not. The lack of consultation about the unfortunate draft report was just the tip of the iceberg—the school really had no say about the shape of the evaluation.

I was involved in the life of the neighborhood school *as an evaluator*, no matter how hard I worked to redefine or deemphasize the role. I speak fluent English, which is the dominant language; I have a Ph.D., which enabled me to be hired; and I get my paycheck from an institution unrelated to either the school or the foundation that supports the evaluation. I could go on; my point is not that I am safe and the school people are not, though that is often true. Rather, I enjoy privileges and influence (sometimes power) that derive from all these other systems. Maybe this means that I can buffer the school from the bureaucracy or interpret its cultural strengths effectively. Certainly it means that I have to acknowledge that my presence is not neutral.

Studying situations in which difference is central also poses an inverse challenge or guideline: the ethnographer must take care not to romanticize the "culture" part of the equation. The neighborhood school at P.S. Y, for example, is located in a predominantly Latino neighborhood. As the ethnographer, I could have perceived and translated the school's bilingualism, its outstanding community programs, and the principal's serving the food of which she said "Did you notice?" strictly in terms of cultural meaning systems, which certainly interest me as a cultural anthropologist.

That interpretation would have diminished, or completely overlooked, the "indigenous" perspective on the same sorts of data. To wit: Latino programming (*and* the principal's lunches) constitute a form of power in the local community. Latino politicians are loyal participants in the school's many festivities and cultural events, and support them generously. Producing useful, contextualized knowledge that makes culture and power central to the research agenda can thus become politically meaningful shifts in how we conceive of research in schools.

The kind of ethnographic evaluation I have reported on exaggerates the postmodern sensibility: Everything we know *is* relational. The balance between culture and power is a key to thinking about this work: Power and powerlessness are abiding relations, often paramount in urban schools; analysis of data from public school research requires investigating the ethnographer's place in the equation.

My third guideline is more practical: We must approach teachers and schools and districts that are working for progressive change, not just to negotiate our own research, but to find out the issues and questions *they* want to have studied. At the disastrous meeting at P.S. Y, the principal and the neighborhood school coordinator could have largely set the agenda, for example, by inviting the outsiders to discuss how the cultural activities that so distinguish their school might be appropriately included in the evaluation. But we would have had to ask.

This third guideline is not intended simply as a payback for a school's generosity; nor do I mean that ethnographers should relinquish their own research questions, or allow the data to become partisan. Data always serve multiple purposes. What can we do with these findings? should be a collaborative question. The external requirements for evaluation of the NSP could be met while *also* investigating practitioners' concerns. If we began to generate projects along these lines, the resources and status brought by university-based researchers could establish the positioned ethnographer's agenda as legitimate, and as has begun to happen with teacher research, broaden the scope of study in which schools might actually choose to participate. Evaluation might then serve bolder purposes than simply sheltering researchers who have good intentions.

One of the cultural anthropologists whose writing offers a vision of the possibilities and politics I seek to illuminate in school research is James Clifford. Read this final quote from him, if you will, as though he were describing the situations that many of us find ourselves in when we do ethnographic evaluation in public schools: "Ultimately my topic is a pervasive condition of off-centeredness in a world of distinct meaning systems, a state of being in culture [school] while looking at culture [school], a form of personal and collective self fashioning" (Clifford, 1988, p. 9).

The historic, world changes that have fed most directly into a new interpretive moment in cultural anthropology are vast and relatively easy to discern, even as they sweep us along with them. (The end of the 19th-century empires; no more grounds for talk of "the field" or "my people.") The changes at home are sometimes harder to perceive, always harder to isolate and identify. They make us feel off-centered. How *can* so many children be so badly served by American schools?

I offer these reflections as a rudimentary map of my own journey to comprehend a positioned ethnography. The map helps me to think about research in schools that could grasp the relations of power and difference that permeate American culture, which themselves create the inequalities that we most want to change. This is a tricky business. If it works, ethnographic evaluation becomes a shared project with the people who are struggling to imagine and create new schools: "a personal and collective self-fashioning" of the education that we want.

References

Burawoy, M., Burton, A., Ferguson, A. A., Fox, K. J., Gamson, J., Gartrell, N., Hurst, L., Hurzman, C., Salsinger, L., Schiffman, J., & Ui, S. (1991). *Ethnography unbound.* Berkeley: University of California Press.

Clifford, J. (1988). *The predicament of culture.* Cambridge, MA: Harvard University Press.

Comer, J. P. (1980). *School power: Implications of an intervention project.* New York: Free Press.

Fetterman, D. M. (1984). Guilty knowledge, dirty hands, and other ethical dilemmas: The hazards of contract research. In

D. Fetterman (Ed.), *Ethnography in educational evaluation* (pp. 211-236). Beverly Hills, CA: Sage.

Freire, P. (1968). *Pedagogy of the oppressed.* New York: Seabury.

Nader, L. (1969). Up the anthropologist: Perspectives gained from studying. In D. Hymes (Ed.), *Reinventing anthropology* (pp. 284-311). New York: Vintage.

Rosaldo, R. (1989). *Culture and truth: The remaking of social analysis.* Boston: Beacon.

Simon, R., & Dippo, D. (1986). On critical ethnographic work. *Anthropology and Education Quarterly, 17*(4), 195-202.

Index